Praise for Easter Delights
A Collection of Easter Recipes
Cookbook Delights Holiday Series-Book 4

…"Easter, a season rich in symbols, customs, and history, as well as a time for delectable and distinctive traditional dishes and boisterous Easter egg hunts, is easily one of the most enjoyable times of the year. **Easter Delights Cookbook** has fun-filled recipes, as well as facts, customs, and history about this most splendid holiday. You will find the poetry heartwarming and inspirational and the dishes scrumptious, with unique as well as traditional holiday favorites. **Easter Delights** will soon be a favorite in your family for generations to come."…

Mary Scripture
Graphic Designer

…"**Easter Delights** is not only a cookbook, it is a wealth of information about Easter. It includes fascinating facts, folklore, and history of Easter, Easter symbols, poetry, and traditions. It even includes information on caring for your Easter lily.

In addition to all this information, it has a collection of over 240 delicious recipes that will be enjoyed by your family and friends.

This cookbook is a great value for the price and makes a wonderful gift."…

Dr. James G. Hood
Editor

Praise for Easter Delights
A Collection of Easter Recipes
Cookbook Delights Holiday Series-Book 4

..."I always look forward to Easter because it's a holiday that represents renewal, along with the ringing in of Spring!

Easter Delights Cookbook is a wonderful way to supplement the occasion. It's filled with hundreds of flavorful recipes, fun traditions, and interesting facts about the holiday. By adding *Easter Delights* to your cookbook collection, it's sure to help you make some special memories that you'll forever cherish!"...

Kimberly Carter
Publicist

..."Easter is a time for worship. It is a time for friends and family to come together and celebrate the victory over death and a new life under the grace of God through our Lord Jesus Christ.

Easter Delights Cookbook is a wonderful tool to help you plan this time of celebration. With over 240 recipes at your fingertips, you will have all you need to make this a special occasion to remember.

Celebrate this new beginning with a new menu from *Easter Delights Cookbook*."...

Ed Archambeault
Spokane, WA

Praise for Easter Delights
A Collection of Easter Recipes
Cookbook Delights Holiday Series-Book 4

…"**Easter Delights Cookbook** has recipes to suit everyone's taste during that special time of remembrance. The detailed indices are particularly helpful for finding favorite recipes. The author has made this cookbook even more personalized by adding some of her own poetry, which makes it stand out from other, more predictable, cookbooks."…

Allyson Schnabel
Editor, Teacher

…"**Easter Delights** is a cookbook that is destined to become a well-loved classic, filled with over 240 delicious recipes that will make planning for this holiday a breeze. Even at a glance, it is clear that author Karen Hood has chosen recipes that reflect the freshness and vibrancy of Spring, using seasonal ingredients that bring dazzling flavors to life. Cooks of all experience and skill will be thrilled with this book, for it offers both traditional dishes and inspiring new recipes that are laid out in a consistent format that is easy to understand and follow. Whether you want to create an elegant brunch or a satisfying dinner, this cookbook provides everything you need to make your Easter meal a success."…

Kim Saunders

iv

Easter Delights

A Collection of Easter Recipes
Cookbook Delights Holiday Series-Book 4

Karen Jean Matsko Hood

Current and Future Cookbooks
By Karen Jean Matsko Hood

DELIGHTS SERIES

Almond Delights
Anchovy Delights
Apple Delights
Apricot Delights
Artichoke Delights
Asparagus Delights
Avocado Delights
Banana Delights
Barley Delights
Basil Delights
Bean Delights
Beef Delights
Beer Delights
Beet Delights
Blackberry Delights
Blueberry Delights
Bok Choy Delights
Boysenberry Delights
Brazil Nut Delights
Broccoli Delights
Brussels Sprouts Delights
Buffalo Berry Delights
Butter Delights
Buttermilk Delights
Cabbage Delights
Calamari Delights
Cantaloupe Delights
Caper Delights
Cardamom Delights
Carrot Delights
Cashew Delights
Cauliflower Delights
Celery Delights
Cheese Delights
Cherry Delights
Chestnut Delights
Chicken Delights
Chili Pepper Delights
Chive Delights
Chocolate Delights
Chokecherry Delights

Cilantro Delights
Cinnamon Delights
Clam Delights
Clementine Delights
Coconut Delights
Coffee Delights
Conch Delights
Corn Delights
Cottage Cheese Delights
Crab Delights
Cranberry Delights
Cucumber Delights
Cumin Delights
Curry Delights
Date Delights
Edamame Delights
Egg Delights
Eggplant Delights
Elderberry Delights
Endive Delights
Fennel Delights
Fig Delights
Filbert (Hazelnut) Delights
Fish Delights
Garlic Delights
Ginger Delights
Ginseng Delights
Goji Berry Delights
Grape Delights
Grapefruit Delights
Grapple Delights
Guava Delights
Ham Delights
Hamburger Delights
Herb Delights
Herbal Tea Delights
Honey Delights
Honeyberry Delights
Honeydew Delights
Horseradish Delights
Huckleberry Delights
Jalapeño Delights

vi

Jerusalem Artichoke Delights
Jicama Delights
Kale Delights
Kiwi Delights
Kohlrabi Delights
Lavender Delights
Leek Delights
Lemon Delights
Lentil Delights
Lettuce Delights
Lime Delights
Lingonberry Delights
Lobster Delights
Loganberry Delights
Macadamia Nut Delights
Mango Delights
Marionberry Delights
Milk Delights
Mint Delights
Miso Delights
Mushroom Delights
Mussel Delights
Nectarine Delights
Oatmeal Delights
Olive Delights
Onion Delights
Orange Delights
Oregon Berry Delights
Oyster Delights
Papaya Delights
Parsley Delights
Parsnip Delights
Pea Delights
Peach Delights
Peanut Delights
Pear Delights
Pecan Delights
Pepper Delights
Persimmon Delights
Pine Nut Delights
Pineapple Delights
Pistachio Delights
Plum Delights
Pomegranate Delights
Pomelo Delights

Popcorn Delights
Poppy Seed Delights
Pork Delights
Potato Delights
Prickly Pear Cactus Delights
Prune Delights
Pumpkin Delights
Quince Delights
Quinoa Delights
Radish Delights
Raisin Delights
Raspberry Delights
Rhubarb Delights
Rice Delights
Rose Delights
Rosemary Delights
Rutabaga Delights
Salmon Delights
Salmonberry Delights
Salsify Delights
Savory Delights
Scallop Delights
Seaweed Delights
Serviceberry Delights
Sesame Delights
Shallot Delights
Shrimp Delights
Soybean Delights
Spinach Delights
Squash Delights
Star Fruit Delights
Strawberry Delights
Sunflower Seed Delights
Sweet Potato Delights
Swiss Chard Delights
Tangerine Delights
Tapioca Delights
Tayberry Delights
Tea Delights
Teaberry Delights
Thimbleberry Delights
Tofu Delights
Tomatillo Delights
Tomato Delights
Trout Delights

Microwave Delights
Milk Shake and Malt Delights
Panini Delights
Pasta Delights
Pesto Delights
Phyllo Delights
Pickled Food Delights
Picnic Food Delights
Pizza Delights
Preserved Delights
Pudding and Custard Delights
Quiche Delights
Quick Mix Delights
Rainbow Delights
Salad Delights
Salsa Delights
Sandwich Delights
Sea Vegetable Delights
Seafood Delights
Smoothie Delights
Snack Delights
Soup Delights
Supper Delights
Tart Delights
Torte Delights
Tropical Delights
Vegan Delights
Vegetable Delights
Vegetarian Delights
Vinegar Delights
Wildflower Delights
Wine Delights
Winemaking Delights
Wok Delights

GIFTS-IN-A-JAR SERIES
Beverage Gifts-in-a-Jar
Christmas Gifts-in-a-Jar
Cookie Gifts-in-a-Jar
Gifts-in-a-Jar
Gifts-in-a-Jar Catholic
Gifts-in-a-Jar Christian
Holiday Gifts-in-a-Jar
Soup Gifts-in-a-Jar

HEALTH-RELATED DELIGHTS
Achalasia Diet Delights
Adrenal Health Diet Delights
Anti-Acid Reflux Diet Delights
Anti-Cancer Diet Delights
Anti-Inflammation Diet Delights
Anti-Stress Diet Delights
Arthritis Delights
Bone Health Diet Delights
Diabetic Diet Delights
Diet for Pink Delights
Fibromyalgia Diet Delights
Gluten-Free Diet Delights
Healthy Breath Diet Delights
Healthy Digestion Diet Delights
Healthy Heart Diet Delights
Healthy Skin Diet Delights
Healthy Teeth Diet Delights
High-Fiber Diet Delights
High-Iodine Diet Delights
High-Protein Diet Delights
Immune Health Diet Delights
Kidney Health Diet Delights
Lactose-Free Diet Delights
Liquid Diet Delights
Liver Health Diet Delights
Low-Calorie Diet Delights
Low-Carb Diet Delights
Low-Fat Diet Delights
Low-Sodium Diet Delights
Low-Sugar Diet Delights
Lymphoma Health Support Diet Delights
Multiple Sclerosis Healthy Diet Delights
No Flour No Sugar Diet Delights
Organic Food Delights
pH-Friendly Diet Delights
Pregnancy Diet Delights
Raw Food Diet Delights
Sjögren's Syndrome Diet Delights

Soft Food Diet Delights
Thyroid Health Diet Delights

HOLIDAY DELIGHTS
Christmas Delights
Easter Delights
Father's Day Delights
Fourth of July Delights
Grandparent's Day Delights
Halloween Delights
Hanukkah Delights
Labor Day Weekend Delights
Memorial Day Weekend
  Delights
Mother's Day Delights
New Year's Delights
St. Patrick's Day Delights
Thanksgiving Delights
Valentine Delights

HOOD AND MATSKO
FAMILY FAVORITES
Hood and Matsko Family
  Appetizers Cookbook
Hood and Matsko Family
  Beverages Cookbook
Hood and Matsko Family
  Breads and Rolls Cookbook
Hood and Matsko Family
  Breakfasts Cookbook
Hood and Matsko Family
  Cakes Cookbook
Hood and Matsko Family
  Candies Cookbook
Hood and Matsko Family
  Casseroles Cookbook
Hood and Matsko Family
  Cookies Cookbook
Hood and Matsko Family
  Desserts Cookbook
Hood and Matsko Family
  Dressings, Sauces, and
  Condiments Cookbook
Hood and Matsko Family
  Ethnic Cookbook

Hood and Matsko Family
  Jams, Jellies, Syrups,
  Preserves, and Conserves
Hood and Matsko Family
  Main Dishes Cookbook
Hood and Matsko Family,
  Pies Cookbook
Hood and Matsko Family
  Preserving Cookbook
Hood and Matsko Family
  Salads and Salad Dressings
Hood and Matsko Family
  Side Dishes Cookbook
Hood and Matsko Family
  Vegetable Cookbook
Hood and Matsko Family,
  Aunt Katherine's Recipe
  Collection, Vol. I-II
Hood and Matsko Family,
  Grandma Bert's Recipe
  Collection, Vol. I-IV

HOOD AND MATSKO
FAMILY HOLIDAY
Hood and Matsko Family
  Favorite Birthday Recipes
Hood and Matsko Family
  Favorite Christmas Recipes
Hood and Matsko Family
  Favorite Christmas Sweets
Hood and Matsko Family
  Easter Cookbook
Hood and Matsko Family
  Favorite Thanksgiving Recipes

INTERNATIONAL
DELIGHTS
African Delights
African American Delights
Australian Delights
Austrian Delights
Brazilian Delights
Canadian Delights
Chilean Delights
Chinese Delights

Czechoslovakian Delights
English Delights
Ethiopian Delights
Fijian Delights
French Delights
German Delights
Greek Delights
Hungarian Delights
Icelandic Delights
Indian Delights
Irish Delights
Italian Delights
Korean Delights
Kosovo Delights
Macedonia Republic Delights
Mexican Delights
Montenegro Delights
Native American Delights
Polish Delights
Russian Delights
Scottish Delights
Serbian Delights
Slovakian Delights
Slovenian Delights
Sri Lanka Delights
Swedish Delights
Thai Delights
The Netherlands Delights
Yugoslavian Delights
Zambian Delights

REGIONAL DELIGHTS
Glacier National Park Delights
Northwest Regional Delights
Oregon Coast Delights
Schweitzer Mountain Delights
Southwest Regional Delights
Tropical Delights
Washington Wine Country
  Delights
Wine Delights of Walla
  Walla Wineries
Yellowstone National Park
  Delights

SEASONAL DELIGHTS
Autumn Harvest Delights
Spring Harvest Delights
Summer Harvest Delights
Winter Harvest Delights

SPECIAL EVENTS DELIGHTS
Birthday Delights
Coffee Klatch Delights
Super Bowl Delights
Tea Time Delights

STATE DELIGHTS
Alaska Delights
Arizona Delights
Georgia Delights
Hawaii Delights
Idaho Delights
Illinois Delights
Iowa Delights
Louisiana Delights
Minnesota Delights
Montana Delights
North Dakota Delights
Oregon Delights
South Dakota Delights
Texas Delights
Washington Delights

U.S. TERRITORIES DELIGHTS
Cruzan Delights
U.S. Virgin Island Delights

MISCELLANEOUS COOKBOOKS
Getaway Studio Cookbook
The Soup Doctor's Cookbook

BILINGUAL DELIGHTS SERIES
Apple Delights, English-
  French Edition
Apple Delights, English-
  Russian Edition

Apple Delights, English-
Spanish Edition
Huckleberry Delights,
English-French Edition
Huckleberry Delights,
English-Russian Edition
Huckleberry Delights,
English-Spanish Edition

CATHOLIC DELIGHTS SERIES

Apple Delights Catholic
Coffee Delights Catholic
Easter Delights Catholic
Huckleberry Delights Catholic
Tea Delights Catholic

CATHOLIC BILINGUAL DELIGHTS SERIES

Apple Delights Catholic,
English-French Edition
Apple Delights Catholic,
English-Russian Edition
Apple Delights Catholic,
English-Spanish Edition
Huckleberry Delights
Catholic, English-Spanish
Edition

CHRISTIAN DELIGHTS SERIES

Apple Delights Christian
Coffee Delights Christian
Easter Delights Christian
Huckleberry Delights Christian
Tea Delights Christian

CHRISTIAN BILINGUAL DELIGHTS SERIES

Apple Delights Christian,
English-French Edition
Apple Delights Christian,
English-Russian Edition
Apple Delights Christian,
English-Spanish Edition
Huckleberry Delights
Christian, English-Spanish
Edition

FUNDRAISING COOKBOOKS

Ask about our fundraising
cookbooks to help raise
funds for your organization.

The above books are also available in bilingual versions. Please contact Whispering Pine Press International, Inc., for details.

The above list of books is not all-inclusive. For a complete list please visit our website or contact us at:

Whispering Pine Press International, Inc.
Your Northwest Book Publishing Company
P.O. Box 214
Spokane Valley, WA 99037-0214 USA
Phone: (509) 928-8700 | Fax: (509) 922-9949
Email: sales@WhisperingPinePress.com
Publisher Websites: www.WhisperingPinePress.com
www.WhisperingPinePressBookstore.com
Blog: www.WhisperingPinePressBlog.com

Easter Delights

A Collection of Easter Recipes
Cookbook Delights Holiday Series-Book 4

Karen Jean Matsko Hood

Published by:

Whispering Pine Press International, Inc.
Your Northwest Book Publishing Company
P.O. Box 214
Spokane Valley, WA 99037-0214 USA
Phone: (509) 928-8700 | Fax: (509) 922-9949
Email: sales@WhisperingPinePress.com
Websites: www.WhisperingPinePress.com
www.WhisperingPinePressBookStore.com
Blog: www.WhisperingPinePressBlog.com
SAN 253-200X
Printed in the U.S.A.

Published by Whispering Pine Press International, Inc.
P.O. Box 214
Spokane Valley, Washington 99037-0214 USA

For sales outside the United States, please contact the Whispering Pine Press International, Inc., International Sales Department.

Manufactured in the United States of America. This paper is acid-free and 100% chlorine free.

Book and Cover Design by Artistic Design Service, Inc.
P. O. Box 1792
Spokane Valley, WA 99037-1792 USA
www.ArtisticDesignService.com

Library of Congress Number (LCCN): 2014901396

Hood, Karen Jean Matsko
Title: Easter Delights Cookbook: A Collection of Easter Recipes: Cookbook Delights Holiday Series-Book 4

p.cm.

ISBN: 978-1-59808-247-0   case bound
ISBN: 978-1-59808-202-9   perfect bound
ISBN: 978-1-59808-203-6   spiral bound
ISBN: 978-1-59808-204-3   comb bound
ISBN: 978-1-59808-206-7   E-PDF
ISBN: 978-1-59210-381-2   E-PUB
ISBN: 978-1-9434-854-9   E-PRC

First Edition: February 2014
1. Cookery *(Easter Delights Cookbook: A Collection of Easter Recipes: Cookbook Delights Holiday Series-Book 4)* 1. Title

Easter Delights Cookbook
A Collection of Easter Recipes
Cookbook Delights Holiday Series-Book 4

Gift Inscription

To: _____

From: _____

_____

Date: _____

Special Message: _____

_____

_____

_____

_____

_____

_____

*It is always nice to receive a personal note to
create a special memory.*

www.EasterDelightsCookbook.com
www.WhisperingPinePress.com
www.WhisperingPinePressBookstore.com

Dedications

To my husband and best friend, Jim.

To our seventeen children: Gabriel, Brianne Kristina and her husband Moulik Kothari, Marissa Kimberly, Janelle Karina and her husband Paul Turcotte, Mikayla Karlene, Kyler James, Kelsey Katrina, Corbin Joel, Caleb Jerome, Keisha Kalani Hiwot, Devontay Joshua, Kianna Karielle Selam, Rosy Kiara, Mercedes Katherine, Jasmine Khalia Wengel, Cheyenne Krystal, and Annalise Kaylee Marie.

To our grandchild Nola, and our future grandchildren.

To our foster grandchildren: Courtney, Lorenzo, and Leah.

To my brother, Stephen, and his wife, Karen.

To my husband's ten siblings: Gary, Colleen, John, Dan, Mary, Ray, Ann, Teresa, Barbara, Agnes, and their families.

In loving memory of my mom, who passed away in 2007; my dad, who passed away in 1976; and my sister, Sandy, who passed away due to multiple sclerosis in 1999.

To Sandy's three sons: Monte, Bradley, and Derek. To Monte's wife, Sarah, and their children: Liam, Alice, Charlie, and Samuel and their foster children. To Bradley's wife, Shawnda, and their children: Anton, Isaac, and Isabel.

To our foster children past and present: Krystal, Sara, Rebecca, Janice, Devontay Joshua, Mercedes Katherine, Zha'Nell, Makia, Onna, Cheyenne Krystal, Onna Marie, Nevaeh, and Zada, our future foster children, and all foster children everywhere.

To the Court Appointed Special Advocate (CASA) Volunteer Program in the judicial system which benefits abused and neglected children.

To the Literacy Campaign dedicated to promoting literacy throughout the world.

Acknowledgements

The author would like to acknowledge all those individuals who helped me during my time in writing this book. Appreciation is extended for all their support and effort they put into this project.

Deep gratitude and profound thanks are owed to my husband, Jim, for giving freely of his time and encouragement during this project.

Thanks are owed to my children Gabriel, Brianne Kristina and her husband Moulik Kothari, Marissa Kimberly, Janelle Karina and her husband Paul Turcotte, Mikayla Karlene, Kyler James, Kelsey Katrina, Corbin Joel, Caleb Jerome, Keisha Kalani Hiwot, Devontay Joshua, Kianna Karielle Selam, Rosy Kiara, Mercedes Katherine, Jasmine Khalia Wengel, Cheyenne Krystal, and Annalise Kaylee Marie. All of these persons inspire my writing.

Thanks are due to Teresa L. Allen and Sharron Thompson for their assistance in typing this manuscript for publication. Thanks go to Artistic Design Service, Inc. for their assistance in formatting and providing a graphic design of this manuscript for publication. This project could not have been completed without them.

Many thanks are due to members of my family, all of whom were very supportive during the time it took to complete this project. Their patience and support are greatly appreciated.

Happy Easter

Easter Delights Cookbook
Table of Contents

Easter Delights Cookbook
A Collection of Easter Recipes
Cookbook Delights Holiday Series-Book 4

Introduction

Easter is both a religious and special family holiday. What a perfect occasion upon which to design a cookbook! The recipes in this book have been collected around the themes, colors, and symbols of Easter. These recipes are great for Easter, but can also be used every day. We hope you enjoy reading it as well as trying out all the recipes. This cookbook is designed for easy use and is organized into alphabetical sections: appetizers; beverages; bread & rolls; breakfast; cakes; candies; cookies; desserts; dressings; sauces & condiments; jams & jellies; main dishes; pies; preserving; salads; side dishes; soups; and wine & spirits;

Do you enjoy reading about Easter, but most importantly, have fun with those you care about while you are cooking, and be sure to look at the list of current and future cookbooks for other titles in the Delights Series of books that you might desire. If you don't find the subject you are looking for, please email us with your suggestion, for consideration in our list. You may email us at info@WhisperingPinePress.com.

Following is a collection of information and recipes gathered and modified to bring you *Easter Delights Cookbook: A Collection of Easter Recipes, Cookbook Delights Holiday Series-Book 4* by Karen Jean Matsko Hood.

Easter Delights Cookbook
A Collection of Easter Recipes
Cookbook Delights Holiday Series-Book 4

Easter Botanical Classification

Easter Botanical Classification

The most popular plant sought at Easter time is the beautiful Easter lily. It is actually the Madonna lily (*Lilium candidum*, a plant in the genus Lilium, a "true lily". It is native to Asia Minor, forming bulbs at ground level and unlike other lilies, has a basal rosette of leaves through the winter, which die back during the simmer months. It has a leafy flower stem, typically up to a height of 2 to 4 feet tall, that emerge in the late spring and bears fragrant pure white flowers in the summer.

The plants are summer flowering. Most species are deciduous, but *Lilium candidum* bears a basal rosette of leaves for much of the year. Flowers are formed at the top of a single erect stem, with leaves being borne at intervals up the stem.

Lilies are native to the northern temperature regions and in New World they extend from southern Canada through much of the United States. In the Old World they are native across much of Europe, the north Mediterranean, across most of Asia to Japan, south to the mountains in India and south to the Philippines. They are commonly adapted to either woodland habitats, or sometimes to grassland habitats.

Easter Delights Cookbook
A Collection of Easter Recipes
Cookbook Delights Holiday Series-Book 4

Easter Cultivation and Gardening

Easter Lilies

Easter Cultivation and Gardening

Two of the things people most value in the Easter lily is it shape and fragrance. When you are selecting your lily, look for plants of high quality with a visually pleasing shape from all angles. You will want to select plants that are well-balanced and not too tall or too short. A good height is a plant that is twice as tall as the pot it is in.

To enjoy your lily for the longest possible time in your home, there are a few things to look for. The best plant to select is one that has flowers in various stages of bloom, from tight buds to partially open flowers. Look for plants with only one or two blooms that are partly or mostly open. It should have three or more unopened buds of different sizes. Puffy buds will open with a few days. Tighter buds will take a few days longer, giving you a longer period of enjoyment.

When you are selecting your Easter lily, make sure to check over the foliage. A plant with a healthy, active root system will have plentiful, dense foliage that extends clear down to the soil line. Healthy foliage also has a rich, dark green color.

Many lilies are packaged in paper, plastic, or mesh sleeves for protection during shipping. If these protective sleeves are left on too long, the quality of the plants will deteriorate, so check the plants over carefully. Check the soil, also. If it is waterlogged and the plant looks wilted, root rot may have already set in, and the plant will not thrive.

After you get your Easter lily home, it will do best in moderately cool daytime temperatures (60 to 65 degrees F.) with nighttime temperatures slightly cooler. Keep the plant out of drafty areas and away from excess heat or dry areas, like that produced by appliances, heating ducts, or fireplaces. Lilies thrive in bright, indirect natural daylight, but you should avoid placing them in direct, glaring sunlight.

As the blooms mature, the yellow anthers should be removed before they start to shed pollen. Removing the anthers keeps the pollen from staining the white flowers and extends the life of the bloom. As the flowers begin to wither, cut them off to keep the plant attractive.

Easter lilies prefer well-drained soil that is moderately moist. Do not over water. When the soil surface feels dry, water the plant thoroughly. Many of the pots are wrapped in decorative foil. This can trap water, causing your lily to stand in water, which is not healthy. To avoid this problem, remove the decorative cover and take your plant to the sink. To completely saturate the soil, water it thoroughly until water is seeping out the pot's drain holes. Allow the plant to sit for a few minutes, discard the excess water, and replace the decorative cover if you desire.

When the last bloom is withered and cut away, you do not need to dispose of your lily. You can continue to enjoy it in the house in the pot, or you can plant it outside in your garden. In the house, once it is finished blooming, place the pot in a sunny location. Continue to water it thoroughly when needed, and every 6 weeks add one teaspoon of slow-release fertilizer. The pot can be moved outside to a sunny location after danger of frost is past.

If you want to plant your Easter lily outside, wait until all danger of frost has passed. You will need a sunny location that has rich, organic matter in the soil and that is well-drained. You can use a planting mix that drains well or make your own mix using one part soil, one part perlite, and one part peat moss. Good drainage is essential for successful lily growing. To help ensure you have adequate drainage, you can raise the level of the garden bed by adding good soil to the top of the bed.

Plant your Easter lily bulb 3 inches below the ground level, mounding an additional 3 inches of topsoil over the bulb. If you have more than one lily, plant the bulbs at least 12 to 18 inches apart. The hole should be deep enough so that you can place the bulb in with the roots spread out and down, as they would naturally grow. Roots that are bound will not produce a healthy, vigorous plant.

Make sure to gently spread the roots and work your prepared soil around both the bulb and roots to make sure no air pockets remain. Immediately after planting, water the bulb thoroughly. Try not to allow the soil to heave or shift.

When the original plant begins to die back, cut the stems back to the surface of the soil. New growth will soon emerge.

Easter lilies are forced to bloom under greenhouse conditions in March, but they will bloom naturally in the summer. It is possible that you may be able to enjoy a second bloom later in the summer, but it is most likely that you will have to wait until June or July of the following year to see your lilies bloom again. Sometimes lilies that have been forced may need a year to rest and recover before returning to a normal blooming cycle.

Although lilies like their heads in the sun, they like their roots in the shade. Mulching will help conserve moisture as well as keep the soil cool and loose, providing a fluffy medium that is nutritious for the roots. A sound gardening alternative to mulch would be a low ground cover of complementary annuals or perennials that have shallow roots. Violas or primulas are not only good cover, but they are a nice contrast to the stately Easter lily.

In the fall, the foliage will turn yellow. Cut the plant back to soil level. Apply bulb fertilizer or blood meal to the top of the soil around your bulb, carefully working it in without disturbing the bulb.

Easter lily bulbs are hardy even in cold climates. You will need to provide winter protection, though, with a thick, generous layer of mulch. Possible mediums would be straw, pine needles, leaves, pieces of boxes or bags, ground corncobs, or newspaper. In the spring, carefully remove the mulch to allow the new shoots to come up. Begin applying a balanced fertilizer as soon as the new growth appears, and continue to apply it monthly until the lily blooms.

With care your Easter lilies will continue to give you enjoyment for years to come.

Easter Delights Cookbook
A Collection of Easter Recipes
Cookbook Delights Holiday Series-Book 4

Easter Facts

Easter Facts

Easter, the Sunday of the Resurrection, Pascha, or Resurrection Day, is the most important religious feast of the Christian liturgical year. This holiday is observed at some point between late March and late April each year (early April to early May in Eastern Christianity), following the cycle of the moon. It celebrates the resurrection of Jesus, which Christians believe occurred on the third day after his death by crucifixion sometime in the period AD 27 to 33.

Lights, candles, and bonfires mark celebrations in many countries. Roman Catholics traditionally extinguish candles in the church on Good Friday and light them again with the Pascal Candle, or Easter Candle, on Easter Day.

The custom of exchanging eggs began long before Easter was celebrated. It was a custom of the Egyptians and the Persians. They exchanged eggs decorated in spring colors. They believed Earth hatched from an egg, which contributed to this custom. In England, they began writing messages and dates on their eggs and exchanging them with friends and loved ones. In the 1800s, candied eggs were made. They were open on one end, and a scene was put inside. These delightful eggs were used as table centerpieces.

Throughout North America, Australia, and parts of the U.K., the Easter holiday has been partially secularized. Some families participate only in the nonreligious traditions, central to which are decorating Easter eggs on Saturday evening and hunting for them Sunday morning. These eggs have been mysteriously hidden all over the house and garden. According to tradition, the eggs are hidden overnight and other treats are delivered by the Easter Bunny. Children find their Easter baskets filled with eggs waiting for them when they wake up.

Many families in America will attend church services in the morning and then participate in a feast or party in the afternoon. In the U.K., the tradition has boiled down to simply exchanging chocolate eggs on Sunday and possibly having an Easter meal. In the northwest of England, the tradition of rolling decorated eggs down steep hills is still followed. It is also traditional to have hot cross buns.

Today many families celebrate Easter in a completely secular way, as a non-religious holiday. Others find this religious holiday one of the most important spiritual events of their Christian calendar.

Easter Folklore

Easter Folklore

The Easter bunny's visit is based upon a German Legend. The legend goes that a poor woman decorated eggs for her children to find during a famine. At the moment they found them, they looked up to see a big bunny hopping away.

The first Easter baskets were made to look like bird's nests.

Americans celebrate Easter with a large Easter egg hunt on the White House Lawn.

The traditional act of painting eggs is called Pysanka. The custom of giving eggs at Easter time has been traced back to Egyptians, Persians, Gauls, Greeks, and Romans, to whom the egg was a symbol of life.

In medieval times, a festival of egg-throwing was held I church, during which the priest would throw a hard-boiled egg to one of the choir boys. It was then tossed from one choir boy to the next and whoever held the egg when the clock struck 12 was the winner and retained the egg.

Easter is now celebrated (in the words of the Book of Common Prayer) on the first Sunday after the full moon that happens on or after March 21, the Spring Equinox.

Easter Bonnets are a throw back to the days when people denied themselves the pleasure of wearing fine things for the duration of Lent.

Easter Delights Cookbook
A Collection of Easter Recipes
Cookbook Delights Holiday Series-Book 4

Easter History

Easter History

Easter, also known as Pascha (Greek for Passover), the Feast of the Resurrection, the Sunday of the Resurrection, or Resurrection Day, is the most important religious feast of the Christian liturgical year. Easter celebrates the resurrection of Jesus, which his followers believe occurred on the third day after his death by crucifixion sometime in the period AD 27 to 33. In the Roman Catholic Church, Easter is actually an eight-day feast called the Octave of Easter. Easter also refers to the season of the Roman Catholic year, lasting for fifty days, from Easter Sunday through Pentecost.

In Western Christianity, Easter always falls on a Sunday from March 22 to April 25 inclusive. The following day, Easter Monday, is a legal holiday in many countries with predominantly Christian traditions. In Eastern Christianity, Easter falls between April 4 and May 8, based on the Gregorian date. The precise date of Easter has often been a matter for contention.

In the United Kingdom, the Easter Act of 1928 set out legislation to allow the date of Easter to be fixed as the first Sunday after the second Saturday in April. However, the legislation has never been implemented.

At a summit in Aleppo, Syria, in 1997, the World Council of Churches proposed a reform in the calculation of Easter which would have replaced an equation-based method of calculating Easter with direct astronomical observation. This act would have side-stepped the calendar issue and eliminated the difference in date between the Eastern and Western churches. The reform was proposed for implementation starting in 2001, but it has not been adopted by any member body.

After their baptisms, early Christians wore white robes all through Easter week to indicate their new lives. Those who had already been baptized wore new clothes instead to symbolize their sharing a new life with Christ.

In Medieval Europe, churchgoers would take a walk after Easter Mass, led by a crucifix or the Easter candle. Today these walks endure as Easter Parades. People show off their spring finery, including lovely bonnets decorated for spring.

As with many other Christian dates, the celebration of Easter extends beyond the church. Since its origins, it has been a time of celebration and feasting. Today it is commercially important, seeing wide sales of greeting cards and confectionery such as chocolate Easter eggs, marshmallow bunnies, Peeps, and jelly beans.

Despite the religious preeminence of Easter, Christmas is now a more prominent event in the calendar year. Christmas is unrivaled as a festive season, commercial opportunity, and time of family gathering—even for those of no faith. Easter's relatively modest secular observances place it a distant second or third among the secular population where Christmas is so prominent.

Belgium shares the same traditions as North America but sometimes it is said that the Bells of Rome bring the Easter Eggs together with the Easter Bunny. The story goes that the bells of every church leave for Rome on Saturday which is called "Stille Zaterdag" (which means "Silent Saturday" in Dutch). Since the bells are in Rome, the bells do not ring anywhere.

In Norway, in addition to skiing in the mountains and painting eggs for decorating, it is tradition to solve murders at Easter. All the major television channels show crime and detective stories (such as Poirot), magazines print stories where the readers can try to figure out who did it, and many new books are published. Even the milk cartons change to have murder stories on their sides. Another tradition of Easter celebration is Yahtzee games. In Finland and Sweden, traditions include egg painting and small children dressed as witches collecting candy door-to-door, in exchange for decorated pussy willows. This is a result of the mixing of an old Orthodox tradition (blessing houses with willow branches) and the Scandinavian Easter witch tradition.

In Hungary, where it is called Ducking Monday, perfume or perfumed water is often sprinkled in exchange for an Easter egg.

In the Czech Republic, Hungary, and Slovakia, a tradition of whipping is carried out on Easter Monday. In the morning, males whip females with a special handmade whip consisting of eight, twelve, or even twenty-four willow rods and decorated with colored ribbons at the end. It must be noted that while whipping can be painful, the purpose is not to cause suffering. Rather, the purpose is for males to exhibit their attraction to females; unvisited females can even feel offended. The whipped female gives a colored egg to the male as a sign of her thanks and forgiveness. A legend says that females should be whipped in order to keep their health and fertility during the whole next year. In some regions the females can get revenge in the afternoon when they can pour a bucket of cold water on any male. The habit slightly varies across the Czech Republic. A similar tradition existed in Poland, where it is called Dyngus Day, but it is now little more than an all-day water fight.

The Christian festival of Easter incorporates many pagan, or pre-Christian, traditions. The origin of its name is unknown. Scholars believe that it probably comes from *Ēastre*, the Anglo-Saxon name of a Germanic goddess of spring and fertility. This derivation was proposed in the 8th century by English scholar Saint Bede. *Ēastre's* festival was celebrated on the day of the vernal equinox—the first day of spring. Traditions associated with her festival survive today in the Easter rabbit, a symbol of fertility, and in colored Easter eggs. Eggs were originally painted with bright colors to represent the sunlight of spring, and were used in Easter-egg rolling contests or given as gifts.

The giving of eggs at spring festivals was not restricted to Germanic peoples and could be found among the Persians, Romans, Jews, and the Armenians. They were a widespread symbol of rebirth and resurrection and thus might have been adopted from any number of sources.

Such festivals, and the stories and legends that explain their origin, were common in ancient religions. A Greek legend tells of the return of Persephone, daughter of Demeter, goddess of the earth, from the underworld to the light of day; her return symbolized to the ancient Greeks the resurrection of life in the spring after the desolation of winter. Many ancient peoples shared similar legends. Wiccans and other Neo-Pagans continue to hold festivals in celebration of the arrival of spring.

Easter Delights Cookbook
A Collection of Easter Recipes
Cookbook Delights Holiday Series-Book 4

Easter Nutrition and Health

Easter Nutrition and Health

Easter is a religious time of year and food in one form or another is one of the celebrations of this lengthy holiday season, one in which we can continue to incorporate nutrition and health into our daily activities.

In this *Easter Delights Cookbook* we have included many nutritious recipes that incorporate the old-time staples of Easter meals and still use some of the fun recipes that are a favorite with children.

If you are on e of the many folks who entertain during this glorious season, the sections of appetizers, beverages, and salads will be of great assistance to you to ascertain that your guests and families will be served with nutritious and healthy foods for quick get togethers. If you are hosting dinners, the sections on main dishes, soups, side dishes, and others, will give recipes that are hearty, while at the same time keeping in mind the need to replenish the body with healthy and nutritious foods for your meals.

We have even included recipes that help you assist the "Easter Bunny" to complete his work for Easter morning and the traditional egg hunt. Some of the recipes include using up those gathered eggs in a nutritional way. The delicacies from the sections on candies, cookies, cakes, and desserts will be anticipated especially by the young folk as a special treat.

However you celebrate this religious and festive season, be sure to have fun in your celebrations to create some cherished memories for everyone to enjoy.

Did You Know? . . . .

Did you know that the Bermuda, or white trumpet, lily was brought to the United States from Bermuda in the 1880s by Mrs. Thomas P. Sargent of Philadelphia, Pennsylvania?

Easter Delights Cookbook
A Collection of Easter Recipes
Cookbook Delights Holiday Series-Book 4

Poetry

A Collection of Poetry with Easter Themes

Table of Contents

Page

Easter

Do we remember Easter?
   The true meaning of
Easter
that is,
When God
   Does rise, above clouds,
     Smooth in wonder,
Grave in nature.
Thank you
for my salvation
Lord.
In awe I reflect . . .
   But do I really know?

Karen Jean Matsko Hood ©2014
Published in *Easter Delights Cookbook*, 2014
By Whispering Pine Press International, Inc., 2014

Anticipation

Rosebuds unfold to expose the tender inside.
Dewdrops on the vase that wilts,
transform the daisies. Behind the glass
the arrival of baby's breath waits for
rain on the mountain top.
Fresh with frigid waking dew
pine siskins buzz,
croon with the chickadees,
pristine frosty air.

Karen Jean Matsko Hood ©2014
Published in *Easter Delights Cookbook*, 2014
By Whispering Pine Press International, Inc., 2014

Crocus

The lovely color of the crocus
  stirs me from sleep,

Chill from frosty winds.
  Snowdrifts shade sunshine,

Rain arrives and wakes us.
  Daffodil buds, thick with gold.

Hues of brightness christen others
  Still quiet in their beds.

Karen Jean Matsko Hood ©2014
Published in *Easter Delights Cookbook*, 2014
By Whispering Pine Press International, Inc., 2014

Easter Altar

Altar frames Easter lilies,
pink azaleas at the foot,
candle bases elevate.
Flames flicker and
conduct the chorus
to invite canaries
to sing in harmony
with warblers.
Bouquets of ebony tulips
meet fragrant
lilies of the valley,
while incense
rises through high notes,
and black
crows pick
the seeds off
low notes.
Cross and resurrection
one,
redemption,
rooted in
lived
union.

Karen Jean Matsko Hood ©2014
Published in *Easter Delights Cookbook*, 2014
By Whispering Pine Press International, Inc., 2014

Palm Sunday

Five weeks of Lent and then it is
Palm Sunday.
Thousands of people gather in
Groups on the worn square, to
Wait for yellow palms that
Border citrinous green,
Frayed at the edges and
Emits fragrance of immature fronds.
Children stand in line and
Wait for their strands of palm.
They wave yellow strips that
Sway in the cold breeze,
As cleansing rain
Patters down over repentant crowds.
The throng teams forth and sings out
Together
Praises their Messiah
With honor and respect.
"Prepare ye the way of the Lord,..."
sings out the tenor.
Melodic voices follow him to the church
Where the sorrowful congregation
Honor their Lord, and
Pay homage to Jesus.
Grief remembers the end and
Waits for resurrection.
Rain drizzles and stops its sprinkle,
Sharp wind penetrates bones.
Eyes stare forward
Retracing what happened to
Try to herald meaning
Now and here.

Karen Jean Matsko Hood ©2014
Published in *Easter Delights Cookbook*, 2014
By Whispering Pine Press International, Inc., 2014

See the Glory

I want to share the goodness
Of this wonderful world:
Truth, justice, love,
Fragrant roses, daffodils and lilacs,
Velvet petals, and soothing blades of grass.
Fall onto your back
At peace. Look up
at the clouds.
See the glory!

Karen Jean Matsko Hood ©2014
Published in *Easter Delights Cookbook*, 2014
By Whispering Pine Press International, Inc., 2014

Moonlit Sun

How long will be my life?
I asked under the sunlit moon.
It seems I want to trade
My days of the magical
Worker bee with the giant
Sea turtle to bask in the
Hushful moonlit sun.

Karen Jean Matsko Hood ©2014
Published in *Easter Delights Cookbook*, 2014
By Whispering Pine Press International, Inc., 2014

Good Morning

Good morning God.
Help me follow your prophecy
today and all the days.
Help me reflect on Your Bible verse.

Help me listen to Your message and
remind me to read from the Bible.
Let me hear what it is You say to me.
These are my needs upon which to reflect.
Help me listen to Your prophets this morning
    and all mornings.

Karen Jean Matsko Hood ©2014
Published in *Easter Delights Cookbook*, 2014
By Whispering Pine Press International, Inc., 2014

Easter Lily

White petals
Unfold
To expose gold,
While
Fragrance
Fills the air
With
Sweet perfume
And a
Scent that
Invigorates
As a
Reminder
Of
God's Creation,
So
Perfect.

Karen Jean Matsko Hood ©2014
Published in *Easter Delights Cookbook*, 2014
By Whispering Pine Press International, Inc., 2014

Easter Delights Cookbook
A Collection of Easter Recipes
Cookbook Delights Holiday Series-Book 4

Easter Symbols

Easter Symbols

Cross: The cross is the symbol of the Crucifixion, as opposed to the resurrection. The cross is not only a symbol of Easter, but it is more widely used, especially by the Catholic Church, as a year-round symbol of their faith.

Easter Bonnet: An Easter Bonnet is a type of hat that people, especially children, wear to Easter services in church. Modern Easter bonnets for children are usually white, wide-brimmed hats with a pastel-colored satin ribbon around it and tied in a bow. It may also have flowers or other springtime motifs on top, and may match a special dress picked out for the occasion.

Easter Bunny: The Easter bunny has its origin in pre-Christian fertility lore. The Hare and the Rabbit were the most fertile animals known, and they served as symbols of the new life during the spring season. The Easter bunny was introduced to American folklore by the German settlers who arrived in the Pennsylvania Dutch country during the 1700s.

Easter Eggs: Long ago in Persia people used to present each other with eggs at the spring equinox, which for them also marked the beginning of a new year. In Christian times the egg had bestowed upon it a religious interpretation, becoming a symbol of the rock tomb out of which Christ emerged to the new life of His Resurrection.

Easter Lily: The lily is seen as a symbol of purity because of its whiteness and delicacy of form. It also symbolizes innocence and the radiance of the Lord's risen life.

Hot Cross Buns: Hot cross buns are typically eaten on Good Friday and during Lent. Stories abound about the origins of the Hot Cross Bun. Yet, the common thread throughout is the symbolism of the "cross" of icing which adorns the bun itself.

Lamb: The Easter lamb represents Christ and may be seen in pictures and images in the homes of central and eastern European families. Lamb is eaten as the main meal on Easter Sunday in many parts of Eastern Europe.

Easter Delights Cookbook
A Collection of Easter Recipes
Cookbook Delights Holiday Series-Book 4

RECIPES

Appetizers and Dips

Table of Contents

Page

Did You Know? . . . .

Did you know that in Western Christianity, Easter marks the end of the forty days of Lent, a period of fasting and penitence in preparation for Easter which begins on Ash Wednesday?

Zesty Cheese Ball

This makes a hearty cheese ball with the added bacon; omit the bacon for vegetarians. It is a nice addition to your Easter appetizer tray, and it can be made up to several days ahead.

Ingredients:

8   oz. cream cheese, softened
½   c. sour cream
2   c. shredded Swiss cheese, room temperature
2   c. shredded cheddar cheese, room temperature
½   c. finely chopped onion
1   jar pimiento (2 oz.), in its juice, chopped
2   Tbs. dill pickle relish
10   slices bacon, crisp cooked, drained, crumbled
½   c. finely chopped pecans, divided
1   dash salt
1   dash pepper
¼   c. snipped parsley
1   Tbs. poppy seeds
    assorted crackers

Directions:

1. In large bowl beat together cream cheese and sour cream until fluffy.
2. Beat in Swiss cheese, cheddar cheese, onion, undrained pimiento, pickle relish, half the bacon, ¼ cup pecans, salt, and pepper.
3. Cover and chill until firm.
4. Shape into 1 large or 2 small balls on wax paper.
5. In small bowl combine remaining bacon, remaining pecans, parsley, and poppy seeds.
6. Turn mixture out onto clean sheet of wax paper.
7. Roll cheese balls in seed mixture to coat, taking up all of the mixture; wrap and chill.
8. Let stand 30 minutes at room temperature before serving.
9. When ready to serve place on serving dish with crackers on the side.

Yields: 1 large or 2 small balls.

Huckleberry Wings

My sons love chicken wings, and this is an easy variation of the classic chicken wings recipe.

Ingredients:

    1½ c. huckleberry jelly
    ⅓   c. balsamic vinegar
    3   Tbs. soy sauce
    1½ tsp. crushed red pepper
    5   lb. frozen chicken wings, thawed

Directions:

1. Preheat oven to 375 degrees F.
2. Line two baking sheets with aluminum foil.
3. In small saucepan over medium heat, combine jelly, vinegar, soy sauce, and red pepper, stirring until smooth.
4. In large bowl toss wings with half the sauce, then place on baking sheets and bake for 20 minutes.
5. Turn wings and brush with remaining sauce.
6. Bake for 8 to 10 minutes more or until no pink remains in chicken and sauce glazes wings.
7. Serve immediately.

Yields: 6 servings.

Spring Rolls

Another family favorite is spring rolls with dipping sauce. This recipe uses ground meat and dried mushrooms for excellent spring rolls. Make extra, as they will go fast.

Ingredients for spring roll:

¼ lb. lean pork or chicken, cut into very thin strips
2 Tbs. cornstarch
2 Tbs. peanut oil
⅓ c. bamboo shoots, cut to same size and shape as meat
2 lg. dried black Chinese mushrooms, soaked, drained
1 sm. leek or lg. scallion, finely chopped
12 spring roll wraps
1 Tbs. all-purpose flour
1 Tbs. cold water
2-3 Tbs. boiling water
    oil for frying

Ingredients for sauce:

½ Tbs. dark or "black" soy sauce
2 Tbs. light soy sauce
2 Tbs. chicken stock
1 Tbs. peanut oil
5 drops sesame oil
1 Tbs. all-purpose flour
1½ tsp. monosodium glutamate
1 pinch salt

Directions:

1. Sprinkle meat with cornstarch and mix well; let stand a few minutes.
2. Heat peanut oil in wok to very hot; sauté meat, bamboo shoots, mushrooms, and leek for 1 minute.
3. Add sauce ingredients; stir-fry until liquid has evaporated, then add leek.

4. Transfer to plate and set aside to cool.
5. Prepare paste for sealing spring roll wraps by dissolving flour in 1 tablespoon cold water.
6. Add 2 to 3 tablespoons of boiling water and stir.
7. Place some of the filling along lower half of each spring roll wrap.
8. Lift up lower edge, fold over filling, tuck edges at both ends, and roll up neatly, sealing final flap with flour and water paste.
9. Fry rolls in plenty of hot oil at 350 degrees F. until bubbling decreases and rolls are golden brown on outside; turn if necessary to brown evenly.
10. Remove from oil, drain, and serve while still piping hot and crisp.

Stuffed Celery with Cream Cheese

My mom always made celery sticks stuffed with cream cheese, and we loved them. Sprinkle with paprika for color.

Ingredients:

1   bunch celery, cut into 4-in. pieces
16 oz. cream cheese, softened
    paprika for garnish

Directions:

1. Beat cream cheese until smooth.
2. Fill celery pieces with cream cheese.
3. Sprinkle with paprika to add color.
4. Arrange on serving dish, cover, and refrigerate until ready to serve

Hard-Boiled Eggs

Our children enjoy hard-boiled eggs. They make an easy snack and appetizer. Use for deviled eggs, egg salad, or in your favorite recipe.

Ingredients:

> 1-12 eggs, as desired
> > water to cover

Directions:

1. Place eggs in saucepan, and cover to depth of about 1 inch with cold water.
2. Allow 3 minutes for soft, 4 minutes for medium, and 5 minutes for firm cooked. For extra large eggs, allow ½ minute longer; for small eggs, allow ½ minute less.
3. Bring to boiling point, cover pan, and reduce temperature to keep water below simmering point; start to time eggs immediately.
4. To very hard cook eggs, allow 25 minutes for large, adding approximately 3 minutes more for extra large, and deducting 3 minutes for medium. Allow less cooking time for small eggs.
5. To test hard-boiled eggs if you forgot to time them, remove from heat and insert toothpick or small skewer through egg shell to center of yolk
6. If it comes out clean, egg is hard-cooked; otherwise, sprinkle opening liberally with salt, and continue cooking until done.
7. Remove from heat when desired cooking time is reached; put in cold water for 5 minutes to stop cooking.
8. Remove shells and use as you desire.

Spinach Balls

When my husband and I were in college, a friend served these at parties. This is a popular appetizer and a quick snack to serve to unexpected guests during the holiday season, particularly since you can make them ahead and keep them on hand in the freezer.

Ingredients:

    2   pkg. frozen spinach (10 oz. each), chopped, drained
    2   c. herb stuffing mix, crushed
    1   c. butter, melted
    4   green onions, chopped
    3   eggs, beaten
        dash of nutmeg

Directions:

1. Combine all ingredients in large bowl; mix well.
2. Shape into 1-inch balls, cover, and refrigerate or freeze until ready to use.
3. When ready to use, preheat oven to 350 degrees F.
4. Set balls on greased baking sheet, and bake for 10 to 15 minutes or until golden brown.
5. Remove from oven, and place on serving plate until cooled to warm.
6. Serve at room temperature with sweet hot mustard sauce.

Did You Know? . . . .

Did you know that in Norway, in addition to cross-country skiing in the mountains and painting eggs for decorating, a contemporary tradition is to solve murder mysteries at Easter?

Empress Chicken Wings

Chicken wings are always popular. These appetizers taste great and make an attractive presentation arranged on a bed of spinach leaves.

Ingredients for wings:

    12 chicken wings
    ½   leek, finely sliced
    1   sm. piece gingerroot, finely sliced
    1   Tbs. rice wine
    1   Tbs. soy sauce
        cornstarch (per directions)
        oil for frying

Ingredients for stock:

    3   c. water
    2   Tbs. soy sauce
    1½   Tbs. rice wine, divided
    2   tsp. sugar
    ½   lb. spinach leaves
    2   Tbs. peanut oil
    1   c. boiling water
    1   pinch salt

Directions for wings:

1. Wash chicken wings well.
2. Cut off tips and reserve.
3. Place chicken wings, leek, and ginger in bowl.
4. Add rice wine and soy sauce; mix well and let stand 30 minutes.
5. Remove chicken wings from marinade, reserving marinade, and pat wings dry with paper towels or cloth.
6. Coat dry wings evenly with cornstarch, and fry lightly in plenty of hot oil.

Directions for stock:

1. In large pan combine water, soy sauce, ½ tablespoon rice wine, and sugar, along with leek and ginger from marinade, and wing tips.
2. Add fried chicken wings, and bring to a boil over high heat.
3. Once liquid has come to a boil, lower heat and cook for about 40 minutes; drain.
4. Meanwhile, wash spinach leaves thoroughly, and stir-fry lightly in 2 tablespoons peanut oil.
5. Season 1 cup of boiling water with pinch of salt and remaining 1 tablespoon rice wine; add spinach and bring back to a boil. As soon as it comes back to a boil, remove spinach and drain.
6. Arrange chicken wings and spinach on serving dish, and serve immediately.

Artichoke Dip

This dip is delicious with crackers or tortilla chips. It is also good on freshly baked bread or bruschetta.

Ingredients:

1   can artichoke hearts, not marinated
4   oz. green chilies, chopped
¾   c. mayonnaise
1½ c. Parmesan cheese
1   clove garlic, minced
    black pepper to taste

Directions:

1. Preheat oven to 350 degrees F.
2. Drain artichoke hearts and break apart.
3. Mix all ingredients together, and place in ovenproof bowl; bake for 30 minutes.

Fried Wontons

These are very popular with all of my children. I double the recipe, and still they disappear.

Ingredients for wontons:

1	lb. ground pork
3	green onions, chopped
⅛	tsp. five spice powder
2	tsp. sesame oil
1	egg yolk
1	tsp. corn or potato starch
1	dash pepper (optional)
1	pkg. wonton skins
1	egg white
	oil for deep-frying

Ingredients for sauce:

½	c. ketchup
3	Tbs. brown sugar
¼	c. red wine vinegar or apple cider vinegar
1	tsp. cornstarch
1	tsp. ground cinnamon
1	dash ground nutmeg
1	dash ground cloves

Directions for wontons:

1. In large mixing bowl combine ground pork, green onions, and spice powder; mix well.
2. Add sesame oil, egg yolk, starch, and pepper to taste.
3. Lay out wonton skins.
4. Place about 1 tablespoon filling in center of each wonton skin.
5. Brush edge with egg white, and fold over diagonally to seal.
6. Deep-fry at 350 degrees F. until light brown.
7. Drain on paper towels and place on serving plate.

Directions for sauce:

1. In saucepan mix together ketchup, brown sugar, and vinegar until blended.
2. Add cornstarch and spices; bring to a boil.
3. Turn heat down and simmer about 2 minutes.
4. Cool and serve with wontons.

Easter Eggs

Our children enjoy hard-boiled eggs, and Easter is really their chance to shine. We have lots of fun dyeing and decorating eggs for that special "Bunny" to deliver. You can use the leftovers for deviled eggs or egg salad.

Ingredients:

vinegar, to assist dye in adhering to cold eggs
hard-boiled eggs
Easter egg dyeing and decorating package or food coloring in assorted shades

Directions:

1. Hard boil eggs according to directions on page 56, but add 1 tablespoon vinegar per dozen eggs to water.
2. Return cooled eggs to egg cartons to keep them from bumping each other and cracking during dyeing and decorating.
3. Follow directions on Easter egg dyeing package.
4. You may also use food coloring to shade desired in each cup; add 1 tablespoon vinegar, fill cup half full with tap water, then proceed with dipping to color.

Creamy Cucumber Dill Dip

This refreshing appetizer with the fresh taste of dill is wonderful when served with chips, crackers, or your favorite fresh vegetables.

Ingredients:

8	oz. cream cheese, softened
1	c. mayonnaise
1	Tbs. lemon juice, freshly squeezed
2	med. cucumbers, peeled, finely chopped
3	Tbs. finely chopped scallions
1	Tbs. snipped fresh dill weed
1	dash cayenne pepper or to taste
	salt
	pepper
	red bell pepper, chopped, for garnish

Directions:

1. Beat cream cheese, mayonnaise, and lemon juice until smooth and creamy.
2. Add cucumbers, scallions, dill, and cayenne, then salt and pepper to taste.
3. Cover tightly and chill until ready to serve.
4. Garnish with additional dill sprigs and chopped red bell pepper if desired.

Yields: 3 cups.

Did You Know?....

Did you know that to determine which Sunday Easter will fall on, a lunar calendar similar to the Hebrew calendar is used?

Clam Dip

Once you make this easy clam dip, you will never purchase a prepackaged one again. It is simple and easy to prepare and tastes delicious. Serve with your favorite chips, vegetables, or sliced French bread. It can be made up to forty-eight hours in advance or stirred up and served immediately.

Ingredients:

6½ oz. clams, minced
8 oz. cream cheese, softened
¼ c. sour cream
½ tsp. Worcestershire sauce
1 tsp. chopped chives
2 Tbs. minced fresh parsley
1 clove garlic, minced
1 dash cayenne pepper
 freshly ground black pepper

Directions:

1. Drain clams, reserving 2 tablespoons juice.
2. Beat juice with cream cheese, sour cream, and Worcestershire sauce.
3. Fold in clams, chives, parsley, garlic, cayenne, and black pepper.
4. Mix together until well blended, then place in serving dish.
5. Refrigerate until ready to serve.

Yields: 2 cups.

Did You Know? . . . .

Did you know that in medieval times eggs were traditionally given at Easter to all servants?

Asparagus with Dipping Sauce

This is a delicious appetizer for the entire family or one for special-occasion entertaining.

Ingredients for asparagus:

48 asparagus spears, cut into 4-in. lengths
3 c. ice
6 c. water
1½ tsp. kosher salt

Ingredients for dipping sauce:

¾ c. sour cream
¼ c. mayonnaise
3 Tbs. chopped red onion
2 Tbs. lemon juice
½ tsp. grated lemon zest
1 Tbs. capers, drained, chopped
2 tsp. dried tarragon
½ tsp. onion powder
½ tsp. sugar
¼ tsp. pepper or to taste

Directions for asparagus:

1. Cook asparagus in steamer basket over boiling water until tender when pierced.
2. Mix ice, water, and kosher salt together in large bowl.
3. Remove asparagus from steamer, and plunge into ice water to stop cooking and turn cold.
4. Transfer to paper towels to drain.
5. Refrigerate.
6. Serve chilled with dipping sauce.
7. Note: Asparagus can be prepared 1 day in advance.

Directions for dipping sauce:

1. Mix sour cream, mayonnaise, onion, and lemon juice together until well blended.
2. Fold in lemon zest, capers, tarragon, and onion powder, blending well.
3. Add sugar and pepper to taste, whisking well.
4. Refrigerate until chilled, about 2 hours.
5. Note: Sauce may be prepared up to 2 days in advance and refrigerated.

Easy Hummus

Our family loves hummus, and this is a very quick and easy recipe that tastes great.

Ingredients:

2   c. canned garbanzo beans
⅔   c. tahini (sesame paste)
1⅔ c. fresh lemon juice
2   cloves garlic
1   tsp. salt
1   dash dried parsley flakes

Directions:

1. Drain garbanzo beans and reserve liquid.
2. Place beans, tahini, lemon juice, and garlic into blender.
3. Purée until smooth, then add salt, parsley, and enough liquid from beans to make dip the consistency preferred.
4. Refrigerate for up to 1 day, until ready to serve with your favorite veggies or crackers.

Yields: 6 servings.

Angel Eggs

We cannot have "deviled eggs" on Easter but "angel eggs." They are perfect and delicious. Be sure to make plenty because these will be enjoyed by all ages. This is a great way to use up all those Easter basket eggs.

Ingredients:

6   lg. hard-boiled eggs (recipe page 56)
1½ tsp. dry mustard
1½ Tbs. mayonnaise
¼   tsp. garlic salt
¼   tsp. onion powder
1   tsp. sweet pickle juice
    paprika for garnish

Directions:

1. Remove shells and cut eggs in half lengthwise; remove yolks.
2. Place yolks in medium bowl and set whites aside.
3. Add mustard, mayonnaise, garlic salt, onion powder, and pickle juice to egg yolks, mixing until well blended.
4. Scoop mixture evenly into hollowed out areas of egg whites, and arrange on serving plate.
5. Sprinkle filled egg halves with paprika.
6. Refrigerate at least 1 hour before serving.
7. Discard any leftover eggs that are not eaten after being set out at room temperature for long periods.

Did You Know?....

Did you know that plastic Easter eggs made their debut in the early 1960s? Now, more than 100 million plastic eggs are purchased for Easter.

Easter Delights Cookbook
A Collection of Easter Recipes
Cookbook Delights Holiday Series-Book 4

Beverages

Table of Contents

Page

Did You Know?....

Did you know that PEEPS® are produced by Just Born, a candy manufacturer based in Bethlehem, Pennsylvania?

Boysenberry Lemonade

Boysenberries and fresh lemons are combined in this delicious drink to add a refreshing touch to Easter.

Ingredients:

    6   lemons, zest reserved
    2   c. water, divided
    1   c. sugar
    ½   c. fresh boysenberries
    2   c. ice
        lemon slices for garnish

Directions:

1. Grate zest from 4 lemons, then squeeze enough juice from these and remaining 2 lemons to measure 1 cup.
2. In saucepan bring to a boil 1 cup water and sugar.
3. Add zest, lemon juice, and remaining 1 cup water; cool mixture.
4. In food processor or blender, purée boysenberries, then stir into lemonade mixture.
5. Pour boysenberry lemonade through sieve into pitcher or other container.
6. Chill, covered, until ready to serve.
7. When ready to serve, pour lemonade over ice in tall, chilled glasses, and garnish with lemon slices.

Yields: 6 cups.

Did You Know? . . . .

Did you know that in France and Belgium, Easter eggs are said to be dropped from the sky by the cloches de Pâques (Easter bells)?

Homemade Chai Tea

Our family loves Chai Tea, and it is best when you make your own mix. Adjust the spices to fit your own taste. My oldest daughter is still in search of the perfect combination of spices to resemble the Chai tea she had when she visited India.

Ingredients:

4	c. water
7	whole cloves
3	cinnamon sticks
7	cardamom pods, cracked open
1	c. loose black tea (use grade to suit taste)
4	c. milk
8	Tbs. sugar or to taste
	ground cinnamon for garnish

Directions:

1. Place water in saucepan with cloves, cinnamon sticks, and cardamom pods; bring to a boil.
2. Remove from heat, add black tea, and let mixture steep for at least 20 minutes, longer if possible.
3. Add milk to tea-spice mixture and heat gently; do not boil.
4. When hot, strain and add sugar.
5. Stir and keep hot until ready to serve.
6. Pour into large mugs, and sift a bit of cinnamon on top.

Did You Know? . . . .

Did you know that the cultivar most widely grown today for greenhouse potted Easter lily production is called "Nellie White"?

Purple Cow

This makes a colorful purple drink for Easter. Your children and child guests will be delighted to see this come to the table!

Ingredients:

    1½ c. cold milk
    3   Tbs. grape juice
    ½   c. vanilla ice cream

Directions:

    1. Combine milk and grape juice in blender.
    2. Add ice cream and mix until smooth.
    3. Pour into chilled glass and serve immediately.

Cherry Spiced Cider

Our family loves spiced ciders, and this makes a delicious and colorful Easter treat.

Ingredients:

    ½   c. maraschino cherry juice
    1   qt. apple cider
    ¾   c. orange juice
    1   cinnamon stick (3-in. length)
    1   strip orange peel (½ x 3 in.)
    3   whole cloves
    3   whole allspice
    16 red maraschino cherries
    8   orange slices, halved

Directions:

1. Put maraschino cherry juice, apple cider, orange juice, cinnamon stick, orange peel, cloves, and allspice in large saucepan; bring to a boil.
2. Reduce heat; simmer 15 minutes.
3. Strain cider to remove spices.
4. Place 2 maraschino cherries and a half orange slice in each of eight mugs.
5. Pour about ⅔ cup spiced cider over top of cherries and orange slice.
6. Serve while warm.

Yields: 8 servings.

Peach Melba

This very tasty drink is a combination of peaches, ice cream, and berries.

Ingredients:

8	oz. peach nectar
2	scoops vanilla ice cream
½	peach, peeled, sliced
3	oz. berries, your choice
	raspberries for garnish

Directions:

1. Combine nectar, ice cream, peach slices, and berries in blender at low speed.
2. Blend until creamy and smooth.
3. Pour into chilled highball glass, and garnish with raspberries.

Roy Rogers

Children enjoy this simple beverage. It is actually just cherry coke, but they like to call it by name.

Ingredients:

    12 oz. cola
    1   shot grenadine
    1   maraschino cherry
        ice

Directions:

1. Combine cola and grenadine in tall glass with ice.
2. Serve garnished with maraschino cherry.

Huckleberry Iced Tea with Cinnamon and Ginger

This makes a refreshing iced tea for Easter Day with the addition of cinnamon and ginger. Serve it with cinnamon sticks for swizzles.

Ingredients:

    6   c. water
    12 huckleberry herbal tea bags
    2   cinnamon sticks (3-in. lengths)
    1   Tbs. minced fresh ginger
    1   c. unsweetened cranberry juice
        sugar
        crushed ice
        cinnamon sticks for swizzles

Directions:

1. Heat water in large saucepan to just before boiling.
2. Add tea bags, cinnamon sticks, and ginger.
3. Remove from heat, cover, and let steep about 15 minutes.
4. Add juice and sugar to taste.
5. Strain tea into pitcher; cover and chill.
6. Pour tea over crushed ice, and serve garnished with cinnamon sticks as swizzles.

Yields: 6 servings.

Orchid Berry Flash

Blueberries, peaches, and yogurt make this a colorful, creamy drink.

Ingredients:

1 fresh peach, peeled, pitted, cut into chunks
1 c. blueberries, fresh or frozen
1 c. vanilla frozen yogurt
2 Tbs. plain yogurt

Directions:

1. Purée peach and blueberries in blender.
2. Add frozen yogurt and plain yogurt, and purée at high speed until smooth.
3. Serve in chilled glasses, topped with a few fresh blueberries if desired.

Springtime Freezy Punch

Tropical fruits make this beverage a wonderful treat that is great for your holiday or special occasion meal, particularly in the spring or summer when you are tired of the long winter and begin dreaming of a nice, long tropical vacation!

Ingredients:

  4   c. mashed bananas
  40 oz. crushed pineapple, undrained
  1   jar maraschino cherries (10 oz.), drained, chopped
  4   c. orange juice
  ½   c. sugar or to taste
      ginger ale

Directions:

  1. Combine bananas, pineapple, cherries, and orange juice in blender; purée until smooth.
  2. Add sugar to taste, then pour into container and freeze until firm.
  3. When ready to serve punch, partially thaw fruit mixture.
  4. Place in punch bowl and break into chunks.
  5. Pour ginger ale over frozen chunks, and let them float in bowl until ready to ladle into chilled glasses.

Did You Know? . . . .

Did you know that in Eastern Christianity, according to the Julian calendar, Easter falls between March 22 and April 25, which on the Western Gregorian calendar is between April 4 and May 8?

Hot Vanilla

This drink is such a refreshing change of pace from hot chocolate. By using fresh vanilla beans, it makes the fragrance and flavor absolutely enticing.

Ingredients:

    1¾ c. milk
    ¼   c. whipping cream
    1   vanilla bean
    1½ tsp. sugar
        ground cinnamon
        Sweetened Whipped Cream (recipe page 175)

Directions:

1. In heavy saucepan combine milk, whipping cream, vanilla bean, and sugar; warm over low heat.
2. When small bubbles appear around sides of pan, remove from heat, and let mixture sit at room temperature for 15 to 20 minutes.
3. Place pan back on stove and warm mixture again, whisking briefly to redistribute skin that forms on milk's surface.
4. Remove vanilla bean; carefully scrape out seeds with sharp knife, and return seeds to milk.
5. Pour into two 8-oz. mugs and top with sprinklings of cinnamon or vanilla bean, adding some whipped cream for extra flavor.

Did You Know? . . . .

Did you know that in Eastern Christianity it was traditional to use up all of the household's eggs before Lent began, which established the tradition of Pancake Day?

Shirley Temple

Children and adults alike seem to enjoy this classic nonalcoholic drink. We serve it on special occasions, and it makes an easy, delicious drink to serve on Easter day.

Ingredients:

    20 oz. ginger ale
    4   oz. grenadine
        ice cubes
        maraschino cherries for garnish

Directions:

1. Divide grenadine evenly among 4 highball glasses, then fill each glass with ice cubes.
2. Add ginger ale over ice.
3. Garnish with a cherry.

Citrus Tea Cooler

Citrus is always refreshing and a pleasant addition to any tea. This is a nice beverage to serve for your Easter lunch.

Ingredients:

    1   Tbs. loose black tea or 3 tea bags
    1½ c. boiling water
    1   c. sugar
    12 ice cubes
    ½   c. fresh lemon juice
    ½   c. fresh orange juice
    1   bottle carbonated lemon-lime drink (28 oz.), chilled

Directions:

1. Place loose tea or tea bags in heatproof bowl.
2. Pour boiling water over tea; let steep for 5 minutes.
3. Remove bags, or strain to remove leaves.
4. Add sugar, and stir until all is dissolved.
5. Place ice cubes in 2-quart serving pitcher.
6. Pour hot tea, lemon, and orange juice over ice cubes.
7. Stir briskly for several seconds until mixture is cold.
8. Stir in chilled lemon-lime carbonated drink.
9. Pour into chilled glasses and serve at once, with or without ice.

Coconut Tropical Cream

This is a popular, refreshing, nonalcoholic tropical drink. It is great for an Easter breakfast or brunch beverage.

Ingredients:

1   oz. cream
¾   oz. coconut cream
1½   oz. cherry juice
1½   oz. pineapple juice
     ice cubes
     maraschino cherry

Directions:

1. Place cream, coconut cream, cherry juice, and pineapple juice into shaker.
2. Add ice cubes and shake well.
3. Strain into chilled large highball glass.
4. Top with maraschino cherry and serve.

Orange Grape Cooler

This is a light-colored drink that is full of flavor for your Easter meal.

Ingredients:

6 oz. frozen orange juice concentrate
1½ c. white grape juice
1½ c. lemon juice
½ c. honey
2 c. water
12 oz. lemon-lime soda

Directions:

1. Combine orange juice, grape juice, lemon juice, and honey in large container.
2. Add water and lemon-lime soda; blend well.
3. When ready to serve, pour into chilled glasses or over ice.

Iced Green Tea

This refreshing drink may be made with or without the sugar, to your preference. Green tea has been touted as good for health because of its antioxidant properties.

Ingredients:

3 Tbs. green tea leaves
3 Tbs. coarsely chopped fresh mint
1 qt. boiling water
1 qt. chilled water
2 Tbs. sugar or to taste
ice cubes
mint sprigs for garnish

Directions:

1. Mix tea, mint, and boiling water in heatproof bowl.
2. Allow to steep about 10 minutes.
3. Strain through wire sieve and discard leaves.
4. Add 1 quart chilled water.
5. Cover bowl, and chill for at least 2 hours or until desired temperature is reached.
6. Add ice and sugar as desired.
7. Garnish with mint sprigs.

Yields: 6 servings.

Coconut Lassi

This is for those of you who enjoy a beverage that is not too sweet.

Ingredients:

2   oz. plain yogurt
2   oz. coconut milk
4   oz. water
1   Tbs. coconut flakes
    crushed ice
    mint leaf

Directions:

1. Place yogurt, coconut milk, water, and coconut flakes in blender.
2. Blend thoroughly, until smooth.
3. Pour into Collins glass about half full of crushed ice.
4. Serve with mint leaf for garnish.

Yields: 1 serving.

Blueberry Yogurt Shake

This is a simple, colorful drink to add to your Easter Day brunch or as a snack anytime.

Ingredients:

    8   oz. blueberry yogurt
    ½   c. frozen blueberries (save 3 or 4 berries for garnish)
    1   tsp. vanilla extract
         honey to taste

Directions:

1. Combine yogurt, blueberries, and vanilla in blender; blend well
2. Add honey to taste and blend until smooth.
3. Pour into chilled 12-ounce glass, and sprinkle a few frozen berries on top.
4. Serve immediately.

Yields: 1 serving.

Mango Lassi

Our tenth child is a beautiful daughter we adopted from India. These Mango Lassies are popular in Indian restaurants. Our family loves them. Enjoy!

Ingredients:

    2   c. mango pulp
    2   c. yogurt
    ½   c. sugar
    1   c. crushed ice

Directions:

1. Place mango pulp, yogurt, and sugar in blender.
2. Blend until smooth.
3. Pour over crushed ice to serve.

Cocoa for Twelve

Try this hot cocoa for a tasty beverage. Serve with colored pastel marshmallows for an added spring touch, or on Easter just for fun!

Ingredients:

½ c. cocoa
½ c. sugar
3 c. water, divided
1 Tbs. vanilla extract
1 qt. evaporated milk or half-and-half
Sweetened Whipped Cream (recipe page 175)
marshmallows (optional)

Directions:

1. In saucepan blend cocoa and sugar; gradually stir in ½ cup water and vanilla to make smooth paste.
2. Add remaining water; bring to a boil, and simmer for 10 minutes.
3. Meanwhile, scald evaporated milk or half-and-half over low heat; stir in cocoa mixture.
4. Cover and let simmer over lowest heat, stirring occasionally, for 30 minutes to mellow.
5. Pour into mugs, and top each serving with colored marshmallows or whipped cream if desired.

Yields: 12 servings.

Hot Spiced Cider

Hot spiced cider fills your home with a magnificent spicy aroma. It is great to have warm on the stove when the children come in from playing. This is also an inviting drink with which to welcome guests on Easter Day.

Ingredients:

    12 c. apple cider
    1   tsp. whole cloves
    ½   tsp. ground nutmeg
    4   sticks cinnamon

Directions:

1. Heat cider, cloves, nutmeg, and cinnamon sticks together in 3-quart saucepan over medium-high heat just to a boil, then reduce heat to simmer.
2. Simmer, uncovered, for 10 minutes.
3. Strain cider mixture to remove spices so cider does not become too strong.
4. Pour into heated mugs and serve while hot.

Did You Know? . . . .

Did you know that in the United Kingdom, the Easter Act of 1928 set out legislation to allow the date of Easter to be fixed as the first Sunday after the second Saturday in April? However, the legislation has not been implemented, although it remains on the statute book and could be implemented subject to approval by the various Christian churches.

Easter Delights Cookbook
A Collection of Easter Recipes
Cookbook Delights Holiday Series-Book 4

Breads and Rolls

Table of Contents

Did You Know? . . . .

Did you know that in Christian times, the egg had bestowed upon it a religious interpretation? It became a symbol of the rock tomb out of which Christ emerged to the new life of His resurrection.

Easter Hot Cross Buns

Try these hot cross buns for your Easter table, or add them to your afternoon tea. They are delicious and will have everyone asking for more.

Ingredients for buns:

¼   c. lukewarm water
½   c. sugar, divided
1   pkg. active dry yeast
3½ c. all-purpose flour
2   Tbs. ground cinnamon
1   tsp. ground nutmeg
¼   tsp. ground cloves
½   tsp. salt
¾   c. warm milk
¼   c. butter, melted
1   egg
1   egg yolk
½   c. currants
¼   c. mixed candied peel, chopped

Ingredients for glaze:

2   Tbs. sugar
2   Tbs. water

Ingredients for icing:

½   c. sifted powdered sugar
2   tsp. water

Directions for buns:

1. In small bowl combine warm water with 1 tablespoon sugar; sprinkle yeast over top, and let stand for 10 minutes or until frothy.
2. Meanwhile, in large bowl blend together remaining sugar, flour, cinnamon, nutmeg, cloves, and salt; make well in center.

3. In small bowl whisk together milk, butter, egg, and egg yolk; pour into well, and then pour in yeast mixture.
4. Add currants and candied peel; using a wooden spoon, stir until soft dough forms.
5. Turn out onto lightly floured surface; knead for 8 minutes or until smooth and elastic.
6. Place in greased bowl, turning to grease all over; cover with plastic wrap, and let rise in warm place for 1 hour or until doubled in bulk.
7. Punch down; turn out onto floured surface, and knead just enough to remove air from dough but not to remove elasticity.
8. Shape into 12-inch log, and then cut into 9 even pieces.
9. Stretch, tuck, and pinch sides of dough all around to meet underneath.
10. Using cupped hand, roll into seamless ball.
11. Place 2 inches apart on greased baking sheet.
12. Cover and let rise for 35 minutes or until impression remains when dough is gently poked.
13. Preheat oven to 400 degrees F.
14. Bake for about 16 minutes or until golden brown.

Directions for glaze:

1. Stir sugar with water in saucepan over medium heat until dissolved.
2. Brush over buns while warm; let cool.

Directions for icing:

1. Stir together powdered sugar and water.
2. Using piping bag fitted with round tip, pipe an icing cross on top of each cooled bun.

Easter Bunny Bread

Children will love these Easter Bunny breads, and they are a great decoration for your holiday table.

Ingredients:

2   pkg. quick-rise instant yeast
½   c. sugar
1½ tsp. salt
4½ c. all-purpose flour, divided
6   Tbs. butter
1   c. water
2   eggs, separated, reserve one egg white
8   chocolate kisses
1   Tbs. powdered sugar
¼   tsp. water
    red food coloring

Directions:

1. Early in the day, combine yeast, sugar, salt, and 1 cup flour.
2. In saucepan over medium heat, heat butter and 1 cup water until hot (125 degrees F.).
3. Using mixer on lowest speed, add liquids gradually to dry ingredients.
4. Beat at medium speed for 2 minutes.
5. Beat in 1 egg white, both egg yolks, and 1 cup flour; continue to beat 2 minutes.
6. Stir in 2¼ cups flour; turn dough onto lightly floured surface, and knead until smooth and elastic, about 5 minutes, working in remaining ¼ cup flour while kneading.
7. Shape dough into ball; cover and let rest 15 minutes.
8. Cut dough into 8 pieces.
9. For each bunny, cut 1 piece of dough in half; shape one half into a ball, placing chocolate kiss in center, for the body. Place on greased cookie sheet.
10. Cut the other half into 2 pieces.

11. Shape one piece into a ball, brush with egg white, and place next to large ball, tucking slightly under for head.
12. From remaining ball, pinch off a small piece for tail, and shape 2 ears from remaining dough.
13. Beat remaining egg white until frothy, then brush tail and ears with egg white to help them stick to body when tucking them slightly under the bunny's body in appropriate places.
14. Brush whole bunny's body with egg white.
15. Continue making bunnies, 4 to a sheet.
16. Preheat oven to 375 degrees F.
17. Bake for 15 minutes or until lightly browned.
18. Remove from oven and lift onto wire rack to cool.
19. Mix powdered sugar with about ¼ teaspoon water and a hint of red food coloring (for pink); use to draw face on bunnies with piping bag.
20. Pipe decoration onto completely cooled bunnies.

Yields: 8 bunnies.

Did You Know? . . . .

Did you know that in Finland, Sweden, and Denmark, traditions include egg painting and small children dressed as witches collecting candy door-to-door, in exchange for decorated pussy willows? This is a result of the mixing of an old Orthodox tradition (blessing houses with willow branches) and the Scandinavian Easter witch tradition.

Caramel Pecan Rolls

My mom used to make these for a special breakfast treat, and they are definitely one of our family's favorites. They freeze well, so you may think about doubling the recipe. Try the "do ahead" version if you are limited in time on the day you would like to make them.

Ingredients for rolls:

> 3½-4 c. all-purpose or bread flour
> ⅓   c. sugar
> 1   tsp. salt
> 2   pkg. active dry yeast, regular or quick
> 1   c. milk, very warm
> ¼   c. butter, softened
> 1   lg. egg
> 2   Tbs. butter

Ingredients for filling:

> 1   c. chopped pecans
> ½   c. raisins
> ¼   c. sugar, granulated or packed brown
> 1   tsp. ground cinnamon

Ingredients for caramel pecan topping:

> 1   c. brown sugar, firmly packed
> ½   c. butter, softened
> ¼   c. corn syrup
> 1   c. pecan halves

Directions for rolls:

1. Mix 2 cups flour, sugar, salt, and yeast in large bowl.
2. Note: If using self-rising flour, omit salt.
3. Add warm milk, ¼ cup butter, and egg.
4. Beat with electric mixer on low speed for 1 minute, scraping bowl frequently.

5. Stir in enough remaining flour to make dough easy to handle.
6. Place dough in greased large bowl, turning dough to grease all sides.
7. Cover bowl loosely with plastic wrap, and let dough rise in warm place about 1½ hours or until doubled in size. (Dough is ready if indentation remains when touched.)
8. Prepare filling ingredients (directions follow).
9. Prepare caramel pecan topping (directions follow).
10. Gently push fist into dough to deflate, and remove from bowl to floured surface.
11. On lightly floured surface flatten dough with hands or rolling pin into 15 x 10-inch rectangle.
12. Spread with 2 tablespoons butter; sprinkle with filling.
13. Roll rectangle up tightly, beginning at long side.
14. Pinch edge of dough into roll to seal.
15. Stretch and shape until even.
16. Cut roll into fifteen 1-inch slices with dental floss or sharp serrated knife.
17. Place slightly apart in pan on top of caramel pecan topping. (If making do-ahead rolls, you will proceed with those directions at this time.)
18. Cover loosely with plastic wrap and let rise in warm place about 30 minutes or until doubled in bulk.
19. Preheat oven to 350 degrees F.
20. Bake for 30 to 35 minutes or until golden brown.
21. Let stand 2 to 3 minutes; immediately turn upside down onto heatproof tray or serving plate.
22. Let stand 1 minute so caramel can drizzle over rolls; remove pan and scrape any syrup remaining in bottom over rolls.
23. Serve warm.

Directions for filling:

1. Combine pecans, raisins, sugar, and cinnamon until well mixed.
2. Set aside until ready to use.

Directions for caramel pecan topping:

1. Heat brown sugar and butter to boiling in 2-quart saucepan, stirring constantly; remove from heat and stir in corn syrup.
2. Pour into ungreased 13 x 9 x 2-inch baking pan.
3. Sprinkle with pecan halves.

Directions for optional do-ahead rolls:

1. After placing slices in pan, cover tightly with plastic wrap or aluminum foil, and refrigerate 4 to 24 hours.
2. Before baking, remove from refrigerator and let rise in warm place about 2 hours or until double. (If some rising has occurred in refrigerator, rising time may be less than 2 hours.) Bake as directed.

Braided Easter Bread

This traditional braided Easter bread can be made ahead. It makes a nice tradition to add to your celebration of Easter.

Ingredients:

2 pkgs. active dry yeast
½ c. warm water
½ c. butter
¾ c. milk
½ c. sugar
2 eggs, lightly beaten
1½ tsp. salt
5 c. all-purpose flour

6	soft-boiled eggs, dyed
1	egg
1	tsp. water
	vegetable oil

Directions:

1. In large mixing bowl dissolve yeast in warm water.
2. Meanwhile, melt butter in saucepan, add milk, and heat until just warm; pour into bowl with yeast.
3. Add sugar, lightly beaten eggs, and salt; stir well.
4. Mix in flour 1 cup at a time until soft dough is formed.
5. Turn dough onto floured surface, adding flour if dough is too sticky to handle; knead until elastic.
6. Place in lightly oiled bowl, cover, and set in warm, draft-free area until doubled in size, about 1 hour.
7. Punch down dough.
8. Divide into 3 equal parts, and roll each piece into a 20-inch-long strand.
9. Lay strands side by side and gently braid them. (To avoid tearing dough, braid from middle out to an end; repeat with other side.)
10. Place woven dough in wreath shape on greased cookie sheet, tucking ends under.
11. Prick eggs on each end and sink them into dough.
12. Cover and let rise until double in size.
13. Beat 1 egg with 1 teaspoon water; brush over dough.
14. Preheat oven to 350 degrees F.
15. Bake for 25 minutes or until golden brown.
16. Remove from oven and cool on wire rack.

Bagels

Bagels are always popular. Serve them cold as bagel sandwiches or toasted with butter. They are delicious with a layer of cream cheese.

Ingredients:

    2   Tbs. cooking oil
    2   Tbs. sugar
    ½   tsp. salt
    1   c. hot water
    2   pkg. active dry yeast
    1   egg
    3¾ c. all-purpose flour, sifted

Directions:

1. In bowl mix oil, sugar, and salt with hot water.
2. When cooled to lukewarm, add yeast to dissolve.
3. Beat egg until frothy; add to above mixture, then mix in flour.
4. Knead dough on lightly floured surface until smooth and elastic.
5. Place in lightly oiled bowl, cover, and let rise in warm place about 20 minutes.
6. Punch dough down; separate into 10 to 12 pieces.
7. With hands, roll out each piece of dough into rope-like length, then overlap ends to join into a circle.
8. Or, cut off ball of dough, flatten into circle, and cut out center with smaller round utensil.
9. Cover and let rise on floured surface.
10. Preheat oven to 400 degrees F.
11. When bagels begin to swell, drop them one at a time into briskly boiling water, and cook until they rise to top and are light.
12. Place on lightly oiled baking sheet, and bake for 15 minutes or until crisp and golden.

English Muffins

Homemade English muffins are the best. They are delicious with homemade jams or jellies.

Ingredients:

    3   c. bread flour, divided
    1   pkg. active dry yeast
    1½ tsp. salt
    1   tsp. sugar
    2   c. warm water, divided

Directions:

1. Place 1 cup flour, yeast, salt, sugar, and 1 cup warm water in large mixing bowl.
2. Mix thoroughly, and let sit until mixture begins to puff up with bubble-like action.
3. Add remaining flour and water slowly to ensure that dough is not too moist.
4. When fully mixed, cover dough with plastic wrap, and let rise in warm place until double in size.
5. Tip dough out onto floured surface, and shape until smooth.
6. Divide dough evenly into 12 pieces, and shape into smooth round balls. (Muffins can be made larger or smaller just by dividing the dough into different numbers of pieces.)
7. Flatten balls of dough into about ¾-inch-thick rounds, then set aside on lightly floured surface to rise until double in size.
8. Heat lightly oiled frying pan to medium heat, and cook each muffin for 5 to 6 minutes on each side, or longer if very fat.
9. Remove and place on wire rack to cool.
10. After cooling, muffins can be split and slowly toasted.
11. Serve with your favorite jelly or jam and butter.

Focaccia

My family enjoys focaccia served hot, but its appeal as an Italian flatbread is preserved whether as a side or main dish. The dough is versatile and makes wonderful breadsticks, which are great with a bit of olive oil and grated Parmesan for dipping. Our whole family loves it with pesto.

Ingredients:

    5-6 c. all-purpose or bread flour (not self-rising)
    4   Tbs. chopped fresh rosemary leaves or 1 Tbs. dried
    2   Tbs. sugar
    2   tsp. salt
    2   pkg. active dry yeast
    10 Tbs. olive or vegetable oil, divided
    2   c. very warm water (120 to 130 degrees F.)
    ¾   c. grated Parmesan cheese

Directions:

1. In large bowl mix 2 cups flour, rosemary, sugar, salt, and yeast.
2. Add 6 tablespoons oil and warm water.
3. Beat with electric mixer on medium speed for 3 minutes, scraping bowl frequently.
4. Stir in enough remaining flour until dough is soft and leaves sides of bowl.
5. Turn dough out onto lightly floured surface; knead 5 to 8 minutes or until dough is smooth and springy.
6. Place dough in large greased bowl, turning dough to grease all sides.
7. Cover bowl loosely with plastic wrap, and let rise in warm place about 30 minutes or until almost double. (Dough is ready if indentation remains when touched.)
8. Grease 2 cookie sheets or 12-inch pizza pans with small amount of oil.
9. Gently push fist into dough to deflate.
10. Divide dough in half.

11. Flatten each half into 10-inch round, lightly coat with cooking spray, and let rise in warm place about 30 minutes or until double.
12. Preheat oven to 400 degrees F.
13. Gently make depressions about 2 inches apart in dough with fingers.
14. Carefully brush with remaining 4 tablespoons olive oil; sprinkle with Parmesan.
15. Bake about 15 to 20 minutes.
16. Remove from oven and serve warm or cool.

Yields: 2 loaves flatbread.

Garlic Bread

Garlic bread is always a welcome Easter dinner addition.

Ingredients:

2   loaves French bread
1   c. butter, softened
3   cloves garlic, crushed
½   c. grated Parmesan cheese

Directions:

1. Preheat oven to 350 degrees F.
2. Slash each loaf of French bread diagonally into 10 thick slices without cutting completely through.
3. Blend butter, garlic, and Parmesan cheese if desired; spread mixture between slices.
4. Wrap each loaf in foil.
5. Bake for 20 to 30 minutes.
6. Remove from oven, and keep wrapped in foil until ready to serve.

Mom's Homemade Whole-Wheat Buns

These old-fashioned homemade buns are still a favorite for the family. They will enhance any meal you choose to serve them with. This dough may also be used for cinnamon rolls.

Ingredients:

¼ c. honey
2 Tbs. active dry yeast
½ c. warm water
2 c. water
¾ c. oil
1 tsp. salt
½ c. brown sugar, firmly packed
1 egg, beaten
6 c. whole-wheat bread flour
   ¼ c. gluten

Directions:

1. In large bowl combine honey, yeast, and ½ cup warm water; let stand for 5 minutes.
2. In another bowl stir together 2 cups water, oil, salt, brown sugar, and egg, mixing well
3. Add this mixture to yeast mixture, blending well.
4. Add 3 cups bread flour and gluten.
5. Mix or beat 5 minutes to develop gluten, for assisting bread to rise.
6. Continue adding 1 cup of flour at a time, just until dough is easy to handle.
7. Turn out onto floured surface and knead until dough is smooth and elastic. (Be careful with flour additions, as too much flour will cause dough to be dry and crumbly.)
8. Cover; set aside in warm area until doubled in bulk.
9. Punch bread down, and form into buns by pinching off ½-cup-size balls of dough.
10. Form each ball until smooth and round, and place on greased cookie sheet.
11. Cover; let rise in warm place until doubled in bulk.

12. Preheat oven to 350 degrees F.
13. Bake for 20 to 25 minutes.

Cornbread

This is a very tasty cornbread that is always good served hot, right out of the pan.

Ingredients:

1 pkg. active dry yeast
¼ c. water, very warm
2 c. milk, scalded
⅓ c. sugar
1 c. butter, softened
1 Tbs. salt
7 c. all-purpose flour, sifted
2 eggs, well beaten
1 c. yellow cornmeal

Directions:

1. Preheat oven to 350 degrees F.
2. In measuring cup sprinkle yeast into very warm water; stir until dissolved.
3. In large mixing bowl combine milk, sugar, butter, and salt.
4. Stir in 3 cups flour, blending well.
5. Stir in eggs, yeast mixture, and cornmeal until well blended.
6. Gradually add and stir in remaining flour.
7. Spoon into greased 13 x 9 x 2-inch baking pan; place in warm area and let rise slightly.
8. Bake for 25 to 30 minutes or until wooden pick inserted in center comes out clean.
9. Remove from oven, cool slightly, and cut into squares to serve warm with butter.

Easter Yeast Rolls

Here is a tasty roll that can be served with any meal during this holiday period. These rolls are easy to make and a delight to eat. They are handy to make because they are started the day before.

Ingredients:

2   pkg. active dry yeast
½   c. warm water
⅔   c. butter, softened
⅔   c. sugar
1½ c. hot water
2   eggs, beaten
1   tsp. salt
6   c. all-purpose flour

Directions:

1. In small bowl mix yeast with ½ cup warm water.
2. In large bowl cream together butter and sugar.
3. Add softened yeast, hot water, eggs, and salt to creamed mixture; blend well.
4. Stir in flour and mix until well blended and slightly sticky; cover with towel for 2 hours.
5. Punch once in middle to deflate; cover with plastic wrap and refrigerate overnight.
6. Shape into rolls and place in greased muffin pans.
7. Let rise for at least 30 minutes.
8. Preheat oven to 375 degrees F.
9. Bake for 15 to 20 minutes or until brown on top and sound hollow when lightly tapped.
10. Remove from oven and serve while warm.

Popovers

I remember the first time I made popovers as a teenager. Try these served hot, right out of the oven. Popovers can also be baked ahead and reheated. When it is time to eat, just reheat on an ungreased cookie sheet at 350 degrees F. for 5 minutes.

Ingredients:

    8   lg. eggs
    4   c. all-purpose flour (not self-rising)
    4   c. milk
    2   tsp. salt

Directions:

1. Preheat oven to 450 degrees F.
2. Generously butter two 12-cup popover pans or twelve 12-ounce custard cups. (If using custard cups, place on cookie sheet to bake.)
3. Beat eggs slightly in medium bowl with fork or wire whisk.
4. Beat in remaining ingredients just until smooth. (Do not overbeat or popovers may not puff as high.)
5. Fill cups about half full.
6. Bake 20 minutes.
7. Reduce oven temperature to 325 degrees F. for popover pan or 350 degrees F. for custard cups.
8. Bake about 20 minutes longer or until deep golden brown.
9. Immediately remove from cups, and pierce each with sharp knife to let steam escape.
10. Serve while hot.

Mom's Whole-Wheat Cinnamon Rolls

This whole-wheat version of the old-fashioned cinnamon roll is a real treat for your family and makes a nice addition to any breakfast.

Ingredients:

    1   batch whole-wheat bun dough (recipe page 96)
    2½ c. brown sugar, firmly packed
    1   c. butter, softened
    ½   c. maple syrup or honey
    2   tsp. ground cinnamon
    1   c. pecans or walnuts, broken in pieces
    1   c. raisins (optional)

Directions:

1. Prepare dough according to recipe.
2. After first rising, punch dough down to deflate, turn out onto lightly floured surface, and pat into rectangle about ½ inch thick.
3. Mix together brown sugar, butter, maple syrup or honey, and cinnamon.
4. Divide mixture into 2 parts to equal ¼ and ¾.
5. Spread the ¼ amount evenly onto bottom of 2 large, shallow, greased baking pans; sprinkle with half the nuts.
6. Spread the ¾ amount over rectangle of dough evenly to ends and completely to one side, leaving about an inch uncovered along one long side.
7. Sprinkle remaining nuts over filling, then sprinkle on raisins if using.
8. Roll dough, starting at side that is totally covered with filling.
9. Pinch long edge gently to seal.
10. Cut dough rolls in half crosswise; using one half for each pan, cut off rolls approximately 1 inch wide and place in rows in greased pans.
11. Cover and let rise in warm place until doubled in bulk.
12. Preheat oven to 375 degrees F.

13. Bake for about 35 minutes.
14. Remove from oven and immediately turn out onto serving platter or pan.
15. Scrape any filling from pan over bottoms of rolls while still hot.
16. These rolls are always delicious when served hot with sweet butter.

Huckleberry Banana Nut Bread

This is moist banana nut bread that is great with the addition of huckleberries.

Ingredients:

1¾ c. sifted all-purpose flour
2 tsp. baking powder
¼ tsp. baking soda
1 pinch salt
⅓ c. butter, softened
⅔ c. sugar
2 eggs
1 c. mashed bananas
1 c. chopped walnuts
1½ c. huckleberries

Directions:

1. Preheat oven to 350 degrees F.
2. Sift together flour, baking powder, soda, and salt.
3. In large bowl cream butter, then gradually beat in sugar until light and fluffy.
4. Add eggs one at a time, mixing well after each addition.
5. Add flour mixture and mashed banana alternately in three parts.
6. Stir in walnuts.
7. Gently fold in huckleberries.
8. Pour into oiled 9 x 5-inch loaf pan.
9. Bake for 50 minutes.
10. Remove from oven; turn out onto wire rack to cool.

Marmalade Oatmeal Bread

This is a delicious bread, made more so by the orange marmalade. It is excellent toasted and freezes well.

Ingredients:

1   c. quick oats
2   c. boiling water
2   pkg. active dry yeast
⅓   c. warm water
½   c. orange marmalade
¼   c. honey
2   Tbs. butter, softened
2½ tsp. salt
6   c. all-purpose flour

Directions:

1. In large bowl cover oats with 2 cups boiling water, and let stand until lukewarm (about 30 minutes).
2. Dissolve yeast in ⅓ cup warm water.
3. Add marmalade and honey to lukewarm oats, and mix well.
4. Stir in softened butter, salt, and yeast.
5. Add flour 2 cups at a time, mixing well after first 2 additions, and kneading in last 2 cups by hand on floured surface.
6. Place dough in greased bowl, turn, cover, and let rise for about 2 hours or until doubled in bulk; punch down.
7. Shape into 2 loaves, and place in 2 large greased loaf pans; let rise until doubled.
8. Preheat oven to 375 degrees F.
9. Bake on lowest rack of oven for about 50 minutes or until golden brown and loaves sound hollow when tapped.
10. Remove from oven; turn out onto wire racks to cool.

Easter Delights Cookbook
A Collection of Easter Recipes
Cookbook Delights Holiday Series-Book 4

Breakfasts

Table of Contents

Did You Know?....

Did you know that the English word "Easter" is derived from the name of the Anglo-Saxon Goddess of the Dawn, "Eastre"?

Asparagus Eggs Benedict

My vegetarian daughter enjoys this version of Eggs Benedict, while the rest of us enjoy the classic version with ham.

Ingredients:

- 1½ lb. asparagus
- ¾ c. butter
- ¾ c. all-purpose flour
- 4 c. milk
- 1 can vegetable broth (14½ oz.)
- ½ c. shredded cheddar cheese
- ½ tsp. salt
- ⅛ tsp. cayenne pepper
- 8 poached eggs (recipe page 113)
- 4 English muffins (recipe page 93)
  freshly grated Parmesan cheese

Directions:

1. Cut asparagus into ½-inch pieces.
2. Cook in boiling water until tender, about 5 minutes; cool.
3. Melt butter in saucepan; stir in flour until smooth.
4. Stir in milk and broth.
5. Bring to a boil; cook and stir for 3 minutes.
6. Add cheese; stir until mixture boils and cheese is melted.
7. Add salt, cayenne pepper, and cooled asparagus.
8. Heat thoroughly, then pour over egg-topped English muffins.
9. Sprinkle Parmesan cheese on top of muffins and serve.

Yields: 8 servings.

Buckwheat Pancakes

My mom used to make buckwheat pancakes for me when I was a child. I loved them with chokecherry syrup, but they are also enjoyable with strawberry syrup.

Ingredients:

1½ c. all-purpose flour
½ c. buckwheat flour
1 tsp. salt
1 tsp. baking soda
1 tsp. baking powder
2 c. buttermilk
2 eggs, lightly beaten
¼ c. honey
1 Tbs. butter, melted
½ c. sunflower seeds, toasted

Directions:

1. In large bowl sift together flours, salt, baking soda, and baking powder.
2. In another bowl whisk together buttermilk, eggs, honey, and butter.
3. Combine wet ingredients with dry, stirring with wooden spoon to combine; batter will be slightly lumpy.
4. Brush hot griddle with oil, then pour ¼ cup of batter onto griddle, leaving 1 inch between pancakes.
5. Immediately sprinkle each pancake with 1 tablespoon sunflower seeds.
6. Cook on one side until bubbles begin to break on surface and underside is brown.
7. Flip and brown; do not overcook.
8. Serve hot with butter and syrup.

Yields: About 8 pancakes.

Crab Cake Eggs Benedict

Crab cakes are a great flavor variation to the traditional Eggs Benedict. Serve this dish with a side of fresh fruit or fresh fruit compote for a nice breakfast or brunch meal.

Ingredients:

- 3 egg yolks
- ½ tsp. salt
- 1 c. unsalted butter, softened
- 4 crab cakes (4 oz. each)
- 1 Tbs. white vinegar
- 4 lg. eggs
- 2 English muffins (recipe page 93)
- 1 Tbs. capers for garnish
  juice of 1 lemon

Directions:

1. Preheat oven to 350 degrees F.
2. Place small, heatproof bowl over pot of steaming water.
3. Add egg yolks, lemon juice, and salt.
4. Using wire whisk, beat butter 1 tablespoon at a time into yolk mixture.
5. When all butter is incorporated, remove bowl from heat and set aside.
6. Place crab cakes on baking sheet, and bake for 15 minutes.
7. Bring small, nonstick pot of water to a simmer; add white vinegar.
8. Crack eggs carefully into shallow bowl, and gently slip eggs into simmering water. (Do not allow water to boil or eggs will fall apart.)
9. Cook until whites are opaque but yolks are not.
10. While eggs are poaching, toast English muffins, and place them on serving plates, open faced.
11. Place a baked crab cake on each muffin half.

12. Lift cooked eggs out of water with slotted spoon, allowing water to drain off before placing on English muffins.
13. Spoon sauce over eggs and garnish with capers.

Yields: 2 to 4 servings.

Poached Eggs in Roman Red Sauce

The red sauce in this recipe for poached eggs makes this a delightfully zesty dish. If you like a creamier sauce, you may add ½ cup of cream to the sauce as it is simmering, before you add the eggs for poaching.

Ingredients:

2   Tbs. olive oil
½   c. chopped onion
½   c. sliced mushrooms, fresh or canned
1   clove garlic, diced
1   can peeled tomatoes
½   c. cream (optional)
4   eggs
     salt and pepper

Directions:

1. In skillet sauté onion, mushrooms, and garlic in olive oil.
2. Add tomatoes, salt, and pepper; heat to simmering, and simmer for 20 minutes.
3. For creamier sauce, stir in cream and heat through.
4. Crack eggs into sauce and let eggs poach.
5. Serve eggs in dish with red sauce and French bread.

Buttermilk Pancakes

There is nothing like waking up to the aroma of old-fashioned buttermilk pancakes in the morning. Top these with strawberry syrup or with strawberries and whipped cream for a tummy-satisfying breakfast treat.

Ingredients:

    3   c. all-purpose flour
    3   Tbs. sugar
    3   tsp. baking powder
    1½ tsp. baking soda
    ¾   tsp. salt
    3   c. buttermilk
    ½   c. milk
    3   eggs
    ⅓   c. butter, melted
        vegetable oil

Directions:

1. In large bowl combine flour, sugar, baking powder, baking soda, and salt.
2. In separate bowl beat together buttermilk, milk, eggs, and melted butter.
3. Heat lightly oiled griddle or frying pan over medium-high heat. (Flick water across surface; when it beads up and sizzles, it is ready.)
4. Pour wet mixture into dry mixture; stir until it is just blended together.
5. Pour ½ cup batter onto griddle.
6. Flip when air bubbles form and break; brown on second side.
7. Repeat with remaining batter.
8. Serve hot with butter and syrup or with fruit and whipped cream.

Chocolate Crêpes

Our family loves crêpes for breakfast, and this makes an interesting variation that our younger chocolate lovers enjoy.

Ingredients:

1⅓ c. all-purpose flour
⅔ c. sugar
2 tsp. unsweetened baking cocoa
3 eggs
½ c. vegetable oil
½ c. milk
various fresh fruits for filling

Directions:

1. Mix all dry ingredients together in mixing bowl.
2. Add all liquid ingredients, and stir until batter is smooth and creamy.
3. Let batter rest in refrigerator until air is settled, about 2 hours.
4. When ready to prepare crêpes, heat crêpe pan over medium heat, and pour ¼ to ⅓ cup batter into hot pan.
5. Rotate pan until batter is cooked through, then turn to cook other side.
6. When done, remove from pan and let cool on rack.
7. Crêpes may be made 1 to 2 days in advance and stored until ready to serve.
8. Fill with seasonal fresh fruits.

Did You Know? . . . .

Did you know that in many historically Christian countries, hot cross buns are traditionally eaten on Good Friday?

Crêpes

This is a favorite of the Hood family! These crêpes are made frequently for special breakfasts. The good thing about this breakfast is that everyone in your family can assemble their own and add their favorite fruits and toppings.

Ingredients:

- 8 lg. eggs
- 2 c. milk
- 5 Tbs. butter, melted
- 2 c. sifted all-purpose flour
- 1 c. sugar
  assorted fresh fruits or jams and jellies
  powdered sugar
  Sweetened Whipped Cream (recipe page 175)

Directions:

1. Mix eggs, milk, butter, flour, and sugar in blender; process until smooth.
2. Heat buttered skillet over medium-high heat; pour in approximately ½ cup batter.
3. When crêpe is looking dry and is lightly browned on bottom, flip to other side and lightly brown.
4. Place on plate, and fill with your favorite fresh fruits or jams and jellies.
5. Roll up and sprinkle with powdered sugar.
6. Serve with a dollop of whipped cream for a delicious breakfast.

Did You Know?....

Did you know that in the U.S., an Easter egg roll is often done on flat ground, pushed along with a spoon?

Easter Breakfast Strata

This is a delicious dish that can be made ahead for your Easter brunch so you do not have to rush on this special day.

Ingredients:

    8   eggs
    3   Tbs. all-purpose flour
    1   Tbs. dry mustard
    3   Tbs. butter, softened
    3   c. milk
    3   c. white bread, cubed
    1½ c. cooked ham, cubed
    1½ c. seasoned breakfast sausage
    1   c. sliced mushrooms, canned or fresh
    ½   lb. cheddar cheese, grated

Directions:

1. In mixing bowl beat together eggs, flour, mustard, butter, and milk; set aside.
2. In lightly greased 13 x 9 x 2-inch pan, layer bread cubes, ham cubes, sausage, mushrooms, and cheese, making 5 layers.
3. Pour egg mixture over layers.
4. Refrigerate at least 6 hours or overnight.
5. Preheat oven to 350 degrees F.
6. Bake for 1 hour and 10 minutes.
7. Let stand at room temperature for 10 minutes before cutting into squares to serve.

Did You Know? . . . .

Did you know that deep-fried chocolate Easter eggs are sold around Easter time in Scottish fish and chips shops?

Soft-Boiled Eggs

Some of my family like their eggs cooked very well done with the yolks hard. Others like the yolks soft for dipping toast or English muffins. This is an easy and foolproof recipe for soft-boiled eggs.

Ingredients:

8   eggs
    salt
    water
    buttered toast

Directions:

1. Place eggs in small pan and cover with salted water; bring water to a boil.
2. From the time water reaches a rolling boil, cook for 3 minutes and 15 seconds.
3. Remove pan from stove, pour out hot water, and run cold water over eggs to stop cooking process.
4. Remove eggs from pan, and dry them off.
5. Cut each egg in half with table knife by giving a sharp, quick hit across center of shell.
6. Break apart, and scoop insides out into serving bowl.
7. Serve with hot, buttered toast cut into small sections for dipping.

Eggs Benedict

My children have made this for me on Mother's Day, and it is an enjoyable classic. They said it was far easier to make than they expected.

Ingredients:

6   slices cooked ham or Canadian bacon
⅓   tsp. butter
3   English muffins, halved, toasted (recipe page 93)
6   eggs, poached (recipe below)
     truffle slices (optional)

Directions:

1. In skillet, sauté ham slices briefly in butter.
2. Place toasted English muffin halves on serving platter.
3. Place ham slice on top each muffin half.
4. Place poached eggs on top ham slices.
5. If desired, serve garnished with truffle slice.

Poached Eggs

Our family enjoys eggs, and these poached ones are a delicious addition to any breakfast.

Ingredients:

3   Tbs. white vinegar
1   tsp. salt
    eggs at room temperature

Directions:

1. Pour water to depth of one inch in skillet; add vinegar and salt, and bring to a boil.
2. Reduce heat immediately to point where boiling stops but it continues to heat.
3. Break eggs one at a time into saucer, slipping each gently into water.
4. Let eggs steep until whites are firm.
5. Using slotted spoon, remove eggs and drain on absorbent paper.
6. Serve while hot in individual dishes with salt, pepper, and butter.
7. Note: Eggs may be poached in advance and reheated briefly in boiling salted water, about 30 seconds, just before serving. This is advantageous if quantities of eggs are to be poached for special occasions.

Classic-Style Eggs Benedict

Our family enjoys eggs, and this recipe works very well. Eat them plain if you are on a low-carb diet.

Ingredients:

6   egg yolks
2   Tbs. cold water
1   c. butter, softened
½   tsp. salt
1   tsp. lemon juice or to taste
   poached eggs (recipe page 113)

Directions:

1. After draining poached eggs, trim with knife or cookie cutter; set aside and keep warm.
2. To make hollandaise sauce, combine egg yolks and water in top of double boiler, and beat with wire whisk over hot (not boiling) water until fluffy.
3. Add a few spoonfuls of butter to mixture, and beat continually until butter has melted and sauce starts to thicken. (Care should be taken that water in bottom of double boiler never boils.)
4. Continue adding butter, bit by bit, stirring constantly.
5. Add salt and lemon juice.
6. For lighter texture, beat in 1 tablespoon hot water if desired.
7. Serve poached eggs topped with sauce.

Did You Know? . . . .

Did you know that each year, thousands of people in New York City wear new clothes to take part in the Easter parade on Fifth Avenue?

Finnish Soufflé

This is a light and fluffy dish that is baked in the oven. It will be puffy in the pan as it is brought to the table straight from the oven. Cut and serve right from the pan, as it will deflate as soon as you cut into it.

Ingredients:

- 4 Tbs. butter
- 4 lg. eggs
- 2 c. milk
- 2 . sugar
- ½ c. all-purpose flour
- ½ tsp. salt
- ½ tsp. vanilla extract

Directions:

1. Preheat oven to 450 degrees F.
2. Melt butter in 13 x 9 x 2-inch baking pan.
3. Beat together eggs, milk, and sugar.
4. Gradually add flour, salt, and vanilla; beat together until creamy.
5. Pour batter on top of butter in pan, and bake for 18 to 23 minutes.
6. Remove from oven, and let stand for about 5 minutes before cutting into squares.
7. Serve hot with maple syrup, jam, or butter.

Did You Know? . . . .

Did you know that today over 95 percent of all bulbs grown for the potted Easter lily market are produced by just ten farms in a narrow coastal region straddling the California-Oregon border, from Smith River, California up to Brookings, Oregon?

Sausage, Egg, and Cheese Casserole

This dish makes a wonderful start to the day. The whole family will enjoy sitting down to eat together and sharing such a tasty dish. This is another dish that is put together the day before, so all you have to do is pop it in the oven for a quick breakfast.

Ingredients:

6   lg. eggs
2   c. milk
1   tsp. salt
1   tsp. dry mustard
2   slices white bread, cubed
1   lb. sausage, browned
1   c. shredded cheddar cheese, sharp or mild
    sour cream for garnish

Directions:

1. Beat eggs, milk, salt, and mustard together, blending well.
2. Grease 13 x 9 x 2-inch baking dish.
3. Layer bread cubes in prepared dish, sprinkle cooked sausage over cubes, then top with cheese.
4. Pour egg mixture over the top, cover, and place in refrigerator overnight.
5. Preheat oven to 350 degrees F.
6. Bake for 45 minutes.
7. Remove from oven, and let stand about 5 minutes before cutting.
8. Serve while hot; top with a dollop of sour cream if desired.

Smoren

This is a traditional family breakfast from our Yugoslavian heritage. Everyone loves this, including all of the children. Sometimes we have it for lunch or dinner.

Ingredients:

1¼ c. sifted all-purpose flour
3 tsp. baking powder
1 Tbs. sugar
½ tsp. salt
1 egg, beaten
1 c. milk
2 Tbs. oil or melted butter
canned plums for topping

Directions:

1. Sift flour, baking powder, sugar, and salt together in large bowl.
2. Mix egg and milk together, and then add to dry ingredients, blending well.
3. Pour into large skillet with about 2 tablespoons oil or butter.
4. Cook over medium heat, stirring and mixing batter until golden brown and of small, pea-sized consistency; or stir less and let pieces stay larger for chewier texture.
5. Remove from heat, place in soup dishes, and spoon plums and juice over each dish. (May also use any other fruit you prefer.)
6. Serve while hot.

Belgian Waffles with Cherry Sauce

These thick, hearty waffles are a family favorite and are very tasty topped with cherry sauce and whipped cream.

Ingredients for cherry sauce:

¼ c. sugar
2 tsp. cornstarch
⅛ tsp. ground cinnamon
½ c. orange juice
2 c. sweet cherries
1 tsp. grated orange peel

Ingredients for waffles:

2 c. all-purpose flour
2 Tbs. sugar
1½ tsp. baking powder
½ tsp. salt
2 c. milk
½ c. butter, melted
4 eggs yolks, beaten
4 egg whites, stiffly beaten
Sweetened Whipped Cream (recipe page 175)

Directions for cherry sauce:

1. In saucepan combine sugar, cornstarch, and cinnamon.
2. Add orange juice, cherries, and orange peel.
3. Bring to a boil over medium-high heat; cook and stir until thickened.

Directions for waffles:

1. Combine flour, sugar, baking powder, and salt.
2. Combine milk, melted butter, and egg yolks; add to dry ingredients, stirring just to moisten.
3. Fold in stiffly beaten egg whites.
4. Bake in waffle iron according to manufacturer's instructions.
5. Serve topped with cherry sauce and whipped cream.

French Toast

My daughter Mikayla likes French toast. This recipe is designed for a large group, but it is easily halved for a smaller family.

Ingredients:

8   eggs
6   c. milk
1   Tbs. butter
24 thick slices French bread
    maple syrup

Directions:

1. Beat eggs in small mixing bowl until light and fluffy; add milk and mix thoroughly.
2. Heat griddle or frying pan to medium-high, and melt butter on surface.
3. Dip both sides of bread slices into egg mixture, and brown on griddle.
4. Turn bread once to cook other side.
5. Place on individual plates, and serve at once with butter and your favorite syrup.

Yields: 12 servings (2 slices each).

Crab Cakes

Crab cakes are very versatile in meal planning, and this recipe is a great one to serve for breakfast, lunch, or even dinner. Serve them with a side of hash browns and eggs to complete your breakfast meal.

Ingredients:

1	stalk celery, finely chopped
1	sm. onion, finely chopped
4	Tbs. olive oil, divided
1	egg, beaten
¼	c. mayonnaise
½	tsp. dry mustard
¼	tsp. garlic powder
¼	tsp. onion powder
¼	tsp. ground red pepper
1½	c. soft French bread crumbs
8	oz. crabmeat, freshly cooked
3	Tbs. finely chopped red sweet pepper
3	Tbs. finely chopped green sweet pepper
	parsley sprigs for garnish

Directions:

1. In skillet sauté celery and onion in 1 tablespoon olive oil until tender; cool slightly.
2. Combine egg, mayonnaise, mustard, garlic powder, onion powder, and ground red pepper in mixing bowl.
3. Add celery mixture, bread crumbs, crabmeat, and red and green sweet peppers; mix well.
4. Shape into 12 cakes.
5. In large skillet over medium heat, cook crab cakes in remaining 3 tablespoons olive oil for 2 to 3 minutes on each side or until lightly browned.
6. Remove from heat and place on serving platter.
7. Garnish with sprigs of parsley.

Cheese Quiche

My vegetarian daughters always request the meatless versions of quiche. Try this one with sautéed mushrooms or sautéed cauliflower.

Ingredients:

- 1 unbaked single-crust pastry shell (recipe page 226)
- 1 Tbs. butter
- 1 sm. onion, finely chopped
- 3 lg. eggs, beaten
- 2¼ c. light cream or whole milk
- 1 tsp. salt
- 14 oz. mozzarella cheese, shredded
- 6 oz. Swiss cheese, sliced
  sautéed mushrooms or cauliflower
  sour cream for garnish

Directions:

1. Preheat oven to 450 degrees F.
2. Sauté onion in butter until translucent and warmed through.
3. In bowl add cream or milk and salt to beaten eggs; blend well.
4. Sprinkle half of mozzarella cheese in bottom of pastry shell, and then add egg mixture.
5. Sprinkle onion into mixture along with remainder of mozzarella cheese.
6. Lay Swiss cheese over top of quiche.
7. Bake 10 minutes, then reduce heat to 325 degrees F. and continue baking for 30 to 50 minutes.
8. When quiche is done, middle has texture of well done omelet (spongy). If it is not spongy in the middle, chances are it will still be watery in the middle.
9. Remove from oven, and let sit for 15 to 20 minutes before serving.
10. Top with sautéed mushrooms or cauliflower and a dollop of sour cream.

Peach Breakfast Biscuits

These light, fluffy biscuits are a great treat for Easter breakfast or a welcome addition to your brunch.

Ingredients:

    2   c. all-purpose flour
    1   Tbs. baking powder
    ¼   tsp. salt
    ⅓   c. butter, softened
    ½   c. plus 2 tsp. milk, divided
    ⅓   c. peach preserves
    2   tsp. sugar
        ⅛ tsp. ground cinnamon

Directions:

1. Preheat oven to 450 degrees F.
2. Stir together flour, baking powder, and salt in medium bowl.
3. Using pastry blender, cut in butter until mixture resembles coarse crumbs.
4. Make well in center.
5. Combine ½ cup milk and preserves in small bowl, then add all at once to dry ingredients.
6. Stir just until dough clings together.
7. Turn out onto lightly floured surface; quickly knead by gently folding and pressing dough 10 to 12 times or until nearly smooth.
8. Lightly roll or pat until ½ inch thick.
9. Cut with floured 2½-inch biscuit cutter, dipping cutter into flour between cuts.
10. Place biscuits 1 inch apart on ungreased baking sheet.
11. Brush tops with remaining 2 teaspoons milk.
12. Combine sugar and cinnamon in small bowl, then sprinkle over biscuits.
13. Bake for 7 to 10 minutes or until golden brown.
14. Serve warm for best flavor.

Easter Delights Cookbook
A Collection of Easter Recipes
Cookbook Delights Holiday Series-Book 4

Cakes

Table of Contents

Page

Did You Know?....

Did you know that Easter is the fundamental and most important festival of the Eastern and Oriental Orthodox? Every other religious festival on their calendars, including Christmas, is secondary in importance to the celebration of the Resurrection of Jesus Christ.

Chocolate Fudge Cake

My son Caleb loves chocolate fudge cake and often requests it for his birthday parties. This cake is very rich, but is easy to make. It has also been a family request for Easter dinner, even with all the other chocolate candy.

Ingredients for fudge cake:

¾ c. butter, melted
1½ c. sugar
1½ tsp. vanilla extract
3 egg yolks
½ c. plus 1 Tbs. baking cocoa
½ c. all-purpose flour
3 Tbs. vegetable oil
3 Tbs. water
¼ c. finely chopped pecans
3 egg whites, room temperature
⅛ tsp. cream of tartar
⅛ tsp. salt

Ingredients for chocolate fudge icing:

1⅓ c. semisweet chocolate chips
½ c. heavy cream or whipping cream
    pecan halves

Directions for fudge cake:

1. Preheat oven to 350 degrees F.
2. Line bottom of 9-inch spring form pan with aluminum foil; butter foil and sides of pan, and set aside.
3. Combine melted butter, sugar, and vanilla in large mixer bowl; beat well.
4. Add egg yolks one at a time, beating well after each addition.

5. Blend in cocoa, flour, oil, and water; beat well.
6. Stir in chopped pecans.
7. In small mixer bowl beat egg whites, cream of tartar, and salt until stiff peaks form.
8. Carefully fold into chocolate mixture.
9. Spoon into prepared pan.
10. Bake 45 minutes or until top begins to crack slightly. (Cake will not be completely done in the center.)
11. Cool for 1 hour.
12. Cover; refrigerate and chill until firm, then remove sides of pan.

Directions for chocolate fudge icing:

1. Prepare icing at serving time.
2. Combine chocolate chips and cream in small saucepan.
3. Cook over low heat, stirring constantly, until chocolate melts and mixture is smooth; do not boil.
4. Cut cake into 12 slices, remove from foil on bottom, and place each slice on a serving plate.
5. Pour icing over each cake slice, allowing it to run down sides of each portion.
6. Garnish with pecan halves.
7. You can also pour icing over entire cake, and garnish with pecan halves; allow cooling.
8. Slice at serving time.

Did You Know? . . . .

Did you know that during the Victorian era, the very conspicuous stamens and pistils of the Easter lily were removed because they were seen as overt symbols of sexuality that might cause the congregation to have impure thoughts?

Blueberry Coffee Cake

Serve this blueberry coffee cake warm with butter and honey. It will be a welcome treat for your Easter meal.

Ingredients for cake:

    1½ c. plus ⅓ c. all-purpose flour
    1   c. sugar
    2½ tsp. baking powder
    1   tsp. salt
    ¼   c. vegetable oil
    ¾   c. milk
    1   egg
    1   c. blueberries

Ingredients for topping:

    ⅓   c. all-purpose flour
    2   c. brown sugar, firmly packed
    ½   tsp. ground cinnamon
    ¼   c. firm butter
    ½   c. blueberries

Directions for cake:

1. Preheat oven to 375 degrees F.
2. Sift together flour, sugar, baking powder, and salt.
3. In medium bowl blend oil, milk, and egg together, then add to flour mixture.
4. Beat thoroughly for 30 seconds, then fold in blueberries just until mixed.
5. Pour into greased, 9-inch round or 8 x 8-inch pan.

Directions for topping:

1. Combine flour, brown sugar, cinnamon, and butter in small bowl.
2. Blend together with fork until size of small peas.
3. Place blueberries over top of batter, then sprinkle sugar mixture over berries and top of batter.

4. Bake for 25 to 30 minutes or until wooden pick inserted in center comes out clean.
5. Remove from oven, and let cool in pan before cutting to serve.

Yields: 8 servings.

Purple Velvet Cake

This is a delightful Easter cake for the kids to enjoy with its purple coloring. Lots of fun and laughter ensue.

Ingredients:

2½ c. all-purpose flour
1½ c. sugar
3   tsp. baking cocoa
1   tsp. baking soda
2   eggs
½   c. oil
1   c. buttermilk
1   tsp. vanilla extract
¼   c. purple food coloring
     Vanilla Butter Cream Frosting (recipe page 129)

Directions:

1. Preheat oven to 350 degrees F.
2. Sift together flour, sugar, cocoa, and soda.
3. In medium bowl beat eggs with fork, then add oil, blending well.
4. Add buttermilk, vanilla, and food coloring; whisk until well mixed.
5. Add sifted dry ingredients, and mix with wire whip until smooth.
6. Pour equally into 2 greased and floured cake pans.
7. Bake for 30 minutes or until wooden pick inserted in center comes out clean.
8. Remove from oven and cool 10 minutes, then turn out onto wire rack to cool completely.
9. Frost with Vanilla Butter Cream Frosting.

Lemon Cake

This dense, lemon-flavored cake is delicious alone or with your favorite berries. This is such a versatile and refreshing cake to serve on Easter Sunday.

Ingredients for cake:

½   lb. unsalted butter, softened
2½ c. sugar
4   extra lg. eggs, room temperature
⅓   c. grated lemon zest
3   c. all-purpose flour
½   tsp. baking powder
½   tsp. baking soda
1   tsp. salt
¾   c. lemon juice, freshly squeezed
¾   c. buttermilk, room temperature.
2   tsp. pure vanilla extract

Ingredients for glaze:

2   c. powdered sugar
3½ Tbs. lemon juice, freshly squeezed

Directions for cake:

1. Preheat oven to 350 degrees F.
2. Grease two 9 x 5-inch loaf pans.
3. In medium bowl with electric mixer, cream butter and sugar together for about 5 minutes or until light and fluffy.
4. With mixer on medium speed, add eggs one at a time, beating well; add lemon zest.
5. In another bowl sift together flour, baking powder, baking soda, and salt.
6. In separate bowl combine lemon juice, buttermilk, and vanilla.
7. Add flour and buttermilk mixtures alternately to creamed mixture, beginning and ending with flour.

8. Divide batter evenly between pans, smooth tops, and bake for 45 minutes to 1 hour, until cake tester comes out clean.
9. Remove from oven and let stand in pan for 10 minutes, and then turn out onto serving plate to cool before adding glaze.

Directions for glaze:

1. Combine powdered sugar and lemon juice.
2. Pour over top of cake before serving.

Vanilla Butter Cream Frosting

This frosting makes a great icing for decorating any kind of cookies and cakes.

Ingredients:

1   lb. powdered sugar, sifted
¼   tsp. salt
¼   c. milk
1   tsp. vanilla extract
⅓   c. butter, softened
     food coloring if desired

Directions:

1. Beat sifted powdered sugar, salt, milk, vanilla, and softened butter until smooth and creamy.
2. Beat in food coloring if desired.
3. If too stiff, beat in a few additional drops of milk.
4. Frost or ice cooled cookies or cake.

Poppy Seed Butter Cake

Poppy seed recipes come from my Yugoslavian and Czechoslovakian ancestry. This version uses butter instead of shortening and also has a simple frosting. If you prefer, leave off the frosting and dust with powdered sugar.

Ingredients for cake:

> 1   c. butter, softened
> 1½ c. sugar
> 1   can ground poppy seed filling
> 4   eggs, separated
> 2   tsp. vanilla extract
> 1   c. dairy sour cream
> 2½ c. all-purpose flour
> 1   tsp. baking soda
> 1   tsp. salt

Ingredients for frosting:

> 4   Tbs. all-purpose flour
> 1   c. milk
> 1   c. butter, softened
> 1   c. sugar
> ⅛   tsp. salt
> 1   tsp. vanilla extract

Directions for cake:

1. Preheat oven to 350 degrees F.
2. Grease and flour 12-cup Bundt pan or 10-inch tube pan, and set aside.
3. Beat butter and sugar in large bowl with electric mixer until light and fluffy.
4. Add poppy seed filling and beat until blended.
5. Beat in egg yolks one at a time, beating well after each addition.

6. Add vanilla and sour cream; beat just until blended.
7. Stir flour, baking soda, and salt until mixed; add to poppy mixture gradually, beating well after each addition.
8. Beat egg whites in separate bowl with electric mixer until stiff peaks form; fold into batter.
9. Spread batter evenly in prepared pan.
10. Bake 60 to 75 minutes or until cake tester inserted in center comes out clean.
11. Remove from oven, and cool in pan on wire rack 10 minutes; invert pan onto wire rack to cool completely.

Directions for frosting:

1. In medium saucepan over medium heat, stir flour and milk together and cook until thick.
2. Let cool to room temperature.
3. Cream butter, sugar, salt, and vanilla.
4. Beat creamed mixture into cooked flour and milk.
5. Spread over cake, or if you prefer, dust cake with powdered sugar.

Did You Know? . . . .

Did you know that the Easter custom of the sunrise religious service was brought to America by Protestant immigrants from Moravia? They held the first such service in Bethlehem, Pennsylvania, in 1741.

Did You Know? . . . .

Did you know that one of the superstitions surrounding Easter is that if it rains on Easter Sunday, it will rain the following seven Sundays?

Sour Cream Chocolate Cake

This is another decadent cake for all the chocolate lovers out there.

Ingredients:

    1   sq. unsweetened chocolate (1 oz.)
    ½   c. hot water
    3   eggs, separated
    1   c. thick sour cream
    1½ c. sugar
    1   tsp. vanilla extract
    1¾ c. all-purpose flour
    ½   tsp. salt
    1   tsp. baking soda

Directions:

1. Preheat oven to 350 degrees F.
2. Melt chocolate in hot water over low heat; cool.
3. In large bowl beat egg yolks with sour cream.
4. Gradually add sugar and beat until thick.
5. Add melted chocolate/water mixture and vanilla to creamed mixture.
6. Sift flour, salt, and baking soda together; add to creamed mixture, mixing well.
7. Stiffly beat egg whites; fold into batter, gently blending.
8. Spoon into wax paper-lined, greased 13 x 9 x 2-inch baking pan.
9. Bake for 45 to 50 minutes or until wooden pick inserted in center comes out clean.
10. Remove from oven, let stand in pan for 10 minutes, then turn out onto wire rack and peel wax paper from bottom.
11. Frost if desired.

Chiffon Cake

My mom made us many chiffon cakes when we were growing up. They are a nice alternative to other cakes, being very moist and having an elegant presentation.

Ingredients:

2½ c. sifted cake flour
1½ c. sugar
3   tsp. baking powder
1   tsp. salt
6   egg yolks, beaten
8   egg whites, very stiffly beaten
¾   c. water
¼   tsp. almond extract
1   tsp. vanilla extract
½   c. vegetable oil
½   tsp. cream of tartar

Directions:

1. Preheat oven to 325 degrees F.
2. Sift flour before measuring, then spoon lightly into measuring cup.
3. Sift flour again with sugar, baking powder, and salt into large bowl.
4. Separate eggs. (Note that this recipe calls for 6 yolks and 8 whites.)
5. Measure water and mix in extracts; add oil and beaten egg yolks.
6. Add liquid ingredients to dry, and beat until smooth, about 1 minute.
7. Beat egg whites and cream of tartar until very stiff or until you are able to cut whites with a knife.
8. Fold batter into beaten whites gradually, mixing in gently after each addition.
9. Spoon into ungreased tube pan, and bake for 65 minutes.
10. Remove from oven; invert onto wire rack to cool.
11. When cake is completely cooled, loosen cake from sides and tube with spatula, and place on serving plate.

Spicy Apple Crunch Cake

This is an easy-to-make, moist apple cake with lots of nuts to add that favorite crunch.

Ingredients for cake:

2	c. sifted all-purpose flour
1	tsp. baking powder
1	tsp. baking soda
1½	tsp. ground cinnamon
⅓	tsp. ground cloves
1	c. brown sugar, firmly packed
½	c. cooking oil
2	eggs, unbeaten
1	c. applesauce
¼	c. milk
1	c. chopped walnuts

Ingredients for topping:

½	c. brown sugar, firmly packed
½	c. chopped walnuts
¼	c. all-purpose flour
1	tsp. ground cinnamon
3	Tbs. butter, softened

Directions for cake:

1. Preheat oven to 350 degrees F.
2. Sift together flour, baking powder, baking soda, cinnamon, and cloves.
3. In large bowl cream brown sugar, oil, and eggs.
4. In another bowl mix applesauce and milk together; add to creamed mixture alternately with dry ingredients, blending well after each addition.
5. Gently fold in walnuts.
6. Spoon batter into 13 x 9 x 2-inch greased pan.
7. Sprinkle topping over batter.
8. Bake for 30 to 45 minutes or until wooden pick inserted in center comes out clean.
9. Remove from oven, and place on wire rack to cool.

10. Slice into squares and serve warm.

Directions for topping:

1. Mix together brown sugar, nuts, flour, and cinnamon.
2. With fork, cut in butter until mixture is crumbly.

Rhubarb Cake

This is one of my husband's favorites. He loves everything made from rhubarb, and this is a moist, easy-to-make cake.

Ingredients:

½   c. butter, softened
1½ c. brown sugar, lightly packed
½   tsp. salt
1   egg, beaten
1   tsp. baking soda
1   c. sour milk
1   tsp. vanilla extract
2   c. all-purpose flour
2½ c. finely chopped rhubarb
½   c. sugar
1   tsp. ground cinnamon
½   c. chopped nuts

Directions:

1. Preheat oven to 350 degrees F.
2. Cream butter; add sugar and mix well.
3. Add salt and beaten egg.
4. Mix soda, milk, and vanilla together in cup.
5. Add milk and flour alternately to creamed mixture, beginning and ending with flour.
6. Fold in rhubarb and mix completely.
7. Pour into greased and floured 13 x 9 x 2-inch pan.
8. Mix together sugar, cinnamon, and nuts; sprinkle over batter.
9. Bake for 45 minutes or until done.

Angel Food Cake

Angel food cake is always welcomes treat and so much better homemade. This is great alone or with your favorite fruit topping along with whipped cream.

Ingredients:

1   c. cake flour
1   c. plus 2 Tbs. all-purpose flour
1½ c. sugar, divided
14 egg whites, room temperature
¾   tsp. salt
1½ tsp. cream of tartar
1½ tsp. vanilla extract
½   tsp. almond extract

Directions:

1. Preheat oven to 350 degrees F.
2. Sift two flours together with ½ cup sugar 6 times.
3. In another bowl beat egg whites until frothy, then add salt, cream of tartar, vanilla, and almond extract.
4. Continue beating until egg whites stay in bowl when inverted.
5. Fold remaining 1 cup sugar into egg whites, 2 tablespoons at a time for 100 folds.
6. Fold flour mixture into egg whites, 2 tablespoons at a time until blended.
7. Spoon batter into ungreased tube pan, and bake for 60 minutes.
8. Remove from oven, and invert on wire rack until cooled.
9. With spatula, loosen cake from sides of pan and place on serving platter ready to slice or frost for serving.

Pineapple and Carrot Cake

This is a delicious and very moist cake. It freezes well, so feel free to make it well ahead of time, and bring it out on Easter to enjoy for dessert after your dinner.

Ingredients:

3   c. all-purpose flour
2   c. sugar
2   tsp. baking soda
½   tsp. salt
1   tsp. ground cinnamon
3   eggs
1   Tbs. cooking oil
2   tsp. vanilla extract
2   Tbs. grated orange peel
½   c. shredded coconut
1½ c. chopped nuts
1   can crushed pineapple (9 oz.)
2½ c. grated raw carrots
½   c. brown sugar, firmly packed

Directions:

1. Preheat oven to 350 degrees F.
2. Sift together flour, sugar, soda, salt, and cinnamon into large bowl.
3. Beat eggs, oil, vanilla, and orange peel together; add to dry ingredients.
4. Beat until smooth, and then fold in coconut, nuts pineapple, and carrots.
5. Spoon into greased and floured tube pan or 13 x 9 x 2-inch baking pan.
6. Sprinkle with brown sugar for added sweetness.
7. Bake for 1 hour and 20 minutes or until wooden pick inserted in center comes out clean.
8. Remove from oven, and cool on wire rack before slicing to serve.

Huckleberry Cake

This is a flavorful combination of huckleberries, pears, and apples. Enjoy the beautiful color and great texture.

Ingredients:

½ c. butter, softened
1   c. sugar
3   eggs
2½ c. all-purpose flour
3   tsp. baking powder
1   tsp. grated orange peel
½ c. milk
½ c. pears, pared, cored, diced
½ c. apples, pared, cored, diced
½ c. dried apricots, diced
2   c. frozen huckleberries, partially thawed
    powdered sugar

Directions:

1. Preheat oven to 375 degrees F.
2. In large mixing bowl cream butter and sugar with electric mixer until light and fluffy.
3. Beat in eggs one at a time, beating well after each addition; set aside.
4. Combine flour, baking powder, and orange peel; mix well.
5. Add flour and milk alternately to creamed mixture, blending well until smooth.
6. Combine all fruits except huckleberries and toss with small amount of flour to lightly coat.
7. Spread half of batter in greased 13-inch tube pan.
8. Fold huckleberries into other fruit, and spoon over batter, then top with remaining batter.
9. Bake for about 1 hour or until golden brown and wooden pick inserted near center comes out clean.
10. Remove from oven and cool on rack for 10 minutes.
11. Carefully invert cake onto serving plate and sprinkle with powdered sugar.
12. Cool completely before slicing to serve.

German Apple Cake

This is a great-tasting, moist cake that can be made ahead of time. It freezes well unfrosted.

Ingredients for cake:

3   eggs
1   c. oil
2   c. sugar
2   c. all-purpose flour
2   Tbs. ground cinnamon
1   tsp. baking soda
4½ c. apples, peeled, thinly sliced
1½ c. chopped nuts

Ingredients for frosting:

8   oz. cream cheese, softened
1   tsp. vanilla extract
3   Tbs. butter, softened
1½ c. powdered sugar

Directions for cake:

1. Preheat oven to 350 degrees F.
2. Beat eggs and oil with mixer until foamy.
3. Add sugar, flour, cinnamon, and baking soda, blending by hand until smooth.
4. Fold in apples and nuts until mixed.
5. Pour into oiled 13 x 9 x 2-inch pan, and bake 50 to 60 minutes.
6. Remove from oven, and turn out onto wire rack to cool before frosting.

Directions for frosting:

1. With mixer combine cream cheese, vanilla, butter, and powdered sugar, beating well.
2. Add food coloring if desired.
3. Place cooled cake on serving plate, and spread with frosting.

Daisy Orange Marble Cake

This is a delicious cake that is especially fun to eat in the spring while sitting on the porch in the sunshine.

Ingredients:

1   c. plus 2 Tbs. cake flour, sifted, divided
1½ c. sugar, divided
1⅓ c. egg whites
1¼ tsp. cream of tartar
¼   tsp. salt
1   c. sugar
1   tsp. grated orange peel
2   Tbs. orange juice
4   egg yolks, well beaten
½   tsp. vanilla extract

Directions:

1. Preheat oven to 350 degrees F.
2. Sift 1 cup flour and ½ cup sugar together.
3. In large mixing bowl beat egg whites with cream of tartar and salt until soft peaks form.
4. Gradually add remaining 1 cup sugar to egg whites, beating until stiff peaks form.
5. Sift ¼ of flour mixture over whites; fold in lightly, then fold in remaining flour mixture by thirds.
6. Divide batter in 2 parts.
7. Add orange peel and juice to egg yolks; beat until very thick and lemon colored.
8. Gently fold egg yolk mixture and remaining 2 tablespoons flour into half of batter.
9. Fold vanilla into other half of batter.
10. Spoon batters alternately into ungreased 10-inch tube pan.
11. Bake for about 35 minutes or until wooden pick inserted in center comes out clean.
12. Remove from oven; invert on wire rack until cool.
13. With spatula, loosen cake from sides of pan, and place on serving platter ready to slice or frost for serving.

Candies

Table of Contents

Page

Did You Know? . . . .

Did you know that the week before Easter is very special in the Christian tradition? The Sunday before is Palm Sunday, and the last three days before Easter are Maundy Thursday or Holy Thursday, Good Friday, and Holy Saturday (sometimes referred to as Silent Saturday). Palm Sunday, Maundy Thursday, and Good Friday respectively commemorate Jesus' entry into Jerusalem, the Last Supper, and the Crucifixion.

Fruit and Nut Easter Eggs

These eggs are both colorful and sweet with the addition of candied fruit. They store for a long period of time, and make great homemade gifts. Try making some ahead of time to beat the Easter day hustle and bustle in the kitchen.

Ingredients:

    2½ c. sugar
    1   c. light corn syrup
    ¾ c. water
    ½ lb. marshmallow cream
    ½ c. shortening, melted
    ¼ c. powdered sugar
    2   c. candied fruit
       nuts
       chocolate candy coating, sufficient for 10 eggs

Directions:

1. In saucepan cook sugar, corn syrup, and water to 265 degrees F. using candy thermometer.
2. Add marshmallow cream and beat until almost firm.
3. Add melted shortening, powdered sugar, candied fruit, and nuts; mix well.
4. Shape eggs with your hands, then dip in melted chocolate candy coating.
5. Eggs will keep for 6 to 8 months, stored between sheets of wax paper in airtight container.

Yields: 10 eggs.

Did You Know? . . . .

Did you know that one of the best-known sunrise services, held at the Hollywood Bowl, began in 1921?

Best Chocolate Fudge

This fudge recipe is the best one I have tried. It is creamy, with great-tasting chocolate, and packed with walnuts. This is another family favorite.

Ingredients:

   2¼ c. top quality chocolate chips
   3   c. fresh walnuts, chopped in large pieces
   1   jar marshmallow cream (9 oz.)
   3   tsp. vanilla extract
   1   c. butter, room temperature
   1   lg. can evaporated milk
   4½ c. sugar

Directions:

1. Butter 13 x 9 x 2-inch pan and cover with wax paper; butter wax paper.
2. In large bowl combine chips, walnuts, marshmallow cream, vanilla, and butter. (Be sure all ingredients are at room temperature).
3. Combine milk and sugar in large pan.
4. Bring to rolling boil on as low a heat as possible.
5. Boil gently for 11 minutes, stirring constantly with wooden spoon. (It may turn brown, so do not be alarmed.)
6. Pour mixture over ingredients in large bowl.
7. Mix quickly without beating.
8. Immediately pour onto wax paper-lined pan as quickly as possible to avoid setting up before spreading out.
9. Cool, then cut into squares.

Chocolate-Covered Marshmallow Easter Eggs

Do not be alarmed by the amount of flour, as it is only used as a mold and may be reused. These are a lot of work, but they are fun to try.

Ingredients:

    25 c. all-purpose flour
    2   Tbs. unflavored gelatin
    ½   c. cold water
    2   c. sugar
    1   c. light corn syrup, divided
    ¾   c. hot water
    2   tsp. vanilla extract
    1   lb. dark chocolate confectionary coating, melted
    2   oz. white candy coating, melted
    1   plastic egg

Directions:

1. Spread 7 cups flour in each of three 13 x 9 x 2-inch baking pans and 4 cups flour in 9-inch square pan, making top even.
2. Press plastic egg halfway into flour to form impression.
3. Repeat 35 times, leaving small amount of space between each impression.
4. In small bowl sprinkle gelatin over cold water; set aside.
5. In large saucepan combine sugar, ½ cup corn syrup, and hot water.
6. Bring to a boil over medium heat, stirring constantly until candy thermometer reads 238 degrees F.
7. Remove from heat; stir in remaining corn syrup.
8. Pour into large mixing bowl.
9. Add reserved gelatin 1 tablespoon at a time, beating on high speed until candy is thick and has cooled to lukewarm.
10. Beat in vanilla.
11. Spoon mixture into egg depressions; dust with flour and let set.

12. Dip each egg shape completely into melted dark chocolate candy coating.
13. Place flat side down on wax paper, and let stand until set.
14. Place melted candy coatings into heavy duty, resealable plastic bags, one for each coating.
15. Cut small hole in bottom corner when ready to use.
16. Drizzle in decorative lines over eggs.
17. When coating is hardened, eggs are ready to serve.
18. Keep eggs layered between wax paper sheets in airtight container for storing.

Green Coconut Nests

Use these nests as an Easter decoration in the middle of each guest's dinner plate.

Ingredients:

1   lb. white chocolate
7   oz. flaked or shredded coconut
    green food coloring
    jelly beans

Directions:

1. In top of double boiler, melt chocolate over hot, not boiling, water.
2. Stir in green food coloring to desired shade.
3. Add coconut and mix together well.
4. Add very small amounts of water to coconut mixture until it thickens enough to hold shapes.
5. Form into small nests by making mounds, then hollowing out with bowl of spoon.
6. Fill nests with jelly beans.

Yields: 8 nests.

Chocolate-Dipped Crispy
Peanut Butter Balls

These candies are quite delicious, easy to make, and enjoyed by children as well as adults.

Ingredients for balls:

½   c. butter
2   c. chunky peanut butter
1   tsp. vanilla extract
1   lb. powdered sugar
3   c. crispy rice cereal

Ingredients for chocolate dip:

2   oz. paraffin wax
1   pkg. chocolate chips (12 oz.)

Directions:

1. Melt butter and while hot, stir in peanut butter and mix well.
2. Add vanilla, powdered sugar, and rice cereal.
3. Allow to cool until safe to mold with hands but not so cool that it is difficult to shape.
4. Form balls with plastic-gloved hands.
5. Melt chocolate and paraffin together over low heat.
6. Dip each ball into melted chocolate mixture with toothpick.
7. Cool on wax paper.
8. Store in refrigerator until ready to serve.

Yields: Approximately 25 servings.

Butterscotch Candy

Butterscotch is a favorite for many, and these candies are no exception. They are a bit like old-fashioned peanut brittle, without the peanuts.

Ingredients:

- 1 c. brown sugar, firmly packed
- ¼ c. light corn syrup
- 1 c. water
- ¼ tsp. salt
- ⅓ c. butter
- ¼ tsp. vanilla extract

Directions:

1. Combine sugar, corn syrup, water, and salt in saucepan; stir over low heat until sugar dissolves.
2. Increase heat and cook until candy thermometer registers 250 degrees F. (firm-ball stage).
3. Add butter and continue cooking, stirring occasionally, until candy thermometer registers 300 degrees F.
4. Remove from stove, add vanilla, and then pour into lightly buttered shallow pan, making layer ¼ inch deep.
5. While warm, score into squares with blunt butter knife.
6. When cool, break into pieces along score lines.
7. Store in cool place in airtight container.

Did You Know? . . . .

Did you know that before World War II, most of the Easter lily bulbs arriving in the United States were imported from Japan?

Chocolate Hay Stacks

This is another easy-to-make candy that is so good it will go fast, so make a big batch.

Ingredients:

6   oz. chocolate chips
6   oz. butterscotch chips
2   tsp. peanut butter
1   c. cashew nuts
4½ c. crunchy Chinese noodles

Directions:

1. In heavy pan stir chocolate chips, butterscotch chips, and peanut butter over low heat until melted.
2. Remove from heat and add cashews and noodles, blending well.
3. Drop by teaspoonfuls onto wax paper.
4. Allow to cool, then store in layers in refrigerator, or wrap individually, and store in airtight container up to 3 months.

Chocolate-Covered Peanut Butter Eggs

Children love chocolate-covered peanut butter eggs, so these will disappear quickly.

Ingredients:

¼   c. butter
¼   c. brown sugar, firmly packed
¾   c. powdered sugar
½   c. creamy peanut butter
1   tsp. vanilla extract
1   pkg. semisweet chocolate chips
2   Tbs. shortening

Directions:

1. In 1-quart microwave-safe bowl, microwave butter and brown sugar on full power for 1 to 1½ minutes, stirring every 30 seconds or until brown sugar is melted.
2. Stir in powdered sugar, peanut butter, and vanilla.
3. Shape by teaspoonfuls into egg shapes; chill.
4. In double boiler or heavy saucepan, melt chocolate chips and shortening over low heat.
5. With wooden pick, dip each egg into chocolate mixture, coating completely.
6. Place on wax paper-lined baking sheets.
7. Store in refrigerator until ready to serve.

Coconut Cream Easter Eggs

This is one of those delicious candies that just melt in your mouth.

Ingredients:

1   med. potato cooked, mashed
16 oz. coconut
¼   tsp. vanilla extract
3   lb. powdered sugar
1   lb. melted chocolate

Directions:

1. Thoroughly mix potato, coconut, and vanilla.
2. Gradually add powdered sugar, and mix until thoroughly blended.
3. Shape into eggs on cookie sheet and let ripen overnight.
4. Next day, dip into melted chocolate.
5. Set eggs onto wax paper to harden.
6. Store in refrigerator until ready to serve, or store in airtight container for longer period.

Divinity

My mom used to make this divinity recipe on holidays and special occasions. She would make pink divinity with nuts for Valentine's Day. Try using different colors to resemble Easter eggs.

Ingredients:

 2½ c. sugar
 ½ c. light corn syrup
 ½ c. water
 2   egg whites, stiffly beaten
 1   tsp. vanilla extract
 ½ c. candied fruit or nuts, chopped
 1-2 drops of red food coloring (optional)

Directions:

1. In heavy saucepan mix sugar, corn syrup, and water; cook and stir over medium-high heat to boiling.
2. Reduce heat to medium, and cook without stirring for 10 to 15 minutes, until candy reaches hard-ball stage.
3. Remove from heat.
4. Gradually pour hot mixture in thin stream over stiffly beaten egg whites while beating on high, about 3 minutes, scraping bowl as you beat mixture.
5. Add vanilla and, if desired, food coloring.
6. Continue beating on high just until candy starts to lose its gloss. (When beaters are lifted, mixture should fall in a ribbon that mounds on itself.) This final beating should take 5 to 6 minutes.
7. Immediately stir in fruits or nuts.
8. Quickly drop mixture by teaspoonfuls onto wax paper.
9. If mixture flattens out, beat for another ½ to 1 minute, then continue to spoon out.
10. If mixture is too stiff to spoon, beat in a few drops hot water until candy is a softer consistency.

Easter Egg Candies

These chocolate Easter egg candies are delicious and slightly moist inside with the addition of coconut.

Ingredients:

1	lb. powdered sugar
2	Tbs. water
1	Tbs. light corn syrup
1	Tbs. butter, softened
1	tsp. vanilla extract
¼	tsp. salt
¼	tsp. almond extract
1	pinch cream of tartar
1⅓	c. flaked coconut
8	sq. semisweet chocolate

Directions:

1. Combine sugar, water, corn syrup, butter, and vanilla.
2. Add salt, almond extract, and cream of tartar; blend well.
3. Stir in coconut.
4. Shape into eggs in desired size and set on wax paper.
5. Melt chocolate in double boiler over low heat.
6. Cool a little, then dribble over eggs.

Did You Know? . . . .

Did you know that the Easter bonnet tradition derives from "olden times," when people dressed up every Sunday to go to church? Ladies purchased new and elaborate designs for particular church services, and in the case of Easter, took the opportunity of the end of Lent to buy luxury items.

Peppermint Taffy

Our kids enjoy making taffy. This candy tastes refreshing and is a great gift for the holidays. It is worth using a candy thermometer to get it correct.

Ingredients:

- 2   c. sugar
- 1   c. light corn syrup
- 1   c. water
- 1½ tsp. salt
- 2   Tbs. butter
- ¼   tsp. oil of peppermint
- 7   drops red food coloring

Directions:

1. In 2-quart saucepan combine sugar, syrup, water, and salt.
2. Cook slowly, stirring constantly, until sugar dissolves.
3. Continue cooking to hard-ball stage (265 degrees F.) without stirring.
4. Remove from heat; stir in butter, peppermint, and food coloring, blending well.
5. Pour into buttered 15½ x 10½ x 1-inch pan.
6. Cool until comfortable to handle.
7. Butter hands; gather taffy into ball.
8. Continuously pull candy until it is light in color and gets hard to pull; cut in fourths, and pull each piece into long strand about ½ inch thick.
9. With buttered scissors, quickly snip into bite-size pieces.
10. Wrap each piece in wax paper to store.

Easter Delights Cookbook
A Collection of Easter Recipes
Cookbook Delights Holiday Series-Book 4

Cookies

Table of Contents

Page

***Did You Know?* . . . .**

Did you know that in Germany eggs used for cooking were not broken? The contents were removed by piercing the end of each egg with a needle and blowing the contents into a bowl. The hollow eggs were dyed and hung from shrubs and trees during Easter Week.

Oatmeal Raisin Cookies

These are great-tasting oatmeal cookies, and you can add chopped nuts for an even better taste.

Ingredients:

¾   c. raisins
¾   c. water
¾   c. butter, melted
1½ c. sugar
1   tsp. vanilla extract
2   eggs
2½ c. all-purpose flour
½   tsp. baking powder
1   tsp. baking soda
1   tsp. ground cinnamon
½   tsp. ground cloves
2   c. rolled oats

Directions:

1. Preheat oven to 400 degrees F.
2. In small saucepan combine raisins and water.
3. Cook over medium heat until just boiling, then remove from heat and set aside to cool; drain and reserve water.
4. In large bowl mix together melted butter, sugar, vanilla, eggs, and raisin water.
5. Sift together flour, baking powder, baking soda, cinnamon, and cloves; stir into egg mixture, then add oatmeal.
6. If the batter seems too runny, let sit for 5 minutes.
7. Drop dough by teaspoonfuls onto oil-sprayed cookie sheet.
8. Bake for 8 minutes.
9. Lift with spatula onto wire racks to cool.

Butter Cookies

These butter cookies are great for a sharing project with children. Use holiday-themed cookie cutters, and have different kinds of sprinkles and candy nonpareils on hand so they can let their imaginations go! Note that the dough needs to be chilled for at least 24 hours, so you will need to plan ahead.

Ingredients:

    3   c. all-purpose flour
    1½ tsp. baking powder
    ½   tsp. salt
    1   c. sugar
    1   c. butter, softened
    1   egg
    3   Tbs. cream
    1   tsp. vanilla extract
        colored candy sprinkles and nonpareils
        frosting

Directions:

1. Sift flour, baking powder, salt, and sugar together.
2. Cut in butter until mixture resembles coarse crumbs.
3. Stir in egg, cream, and vanilla; blend thoroughly. (This usually works best with your hands.)
4. Form dough into flattened ball, wrap, and refrigerate for at least 24 hours or up to several days.
5. Preheat oven to 400 degrees F.
6. Roll dough out on floured surface to about ¼ to ⅛ inch thick.
7. Cut out shapes with cookie cutter, place on cookie sheet, and bake for 5 to 8 minutes.
8. Lift with spatula onto wire racks to cool.
9. Decorate with frosting and different types of sprinkles and candies.

Cream Cheese Sugar Cookies

These delicious, simple cookies can be easily decorated for special occasions. The dough needs to chill for at least 8 hours.

Ingredients:

- 1   c. sugar
- 1   c. butter, softened
- 8   oz. cream cheese, softened
- ½   tsp. salt
- ½   tsp. almond extract
- ½   tsp. vanilla extract
- 1   egg yolk
- 2¼ c. all-purpose flour

Directions:

1. In large bowl combine sugar, butter, cream cheese, salt, extracts, and egg yolk.
2. Beat until smooth, and then stir in flour until well blended.
3. Chill dough at least 8 hours or overnight.
4. Preheat oven to 350 degrees F.
5. On lightly floured surface, roll out dough ⅓ at a time to ⅛-inch thickness, refrigerating remaining dough until ready to use.
6. Cut into desired shapes with lightly floured cookie cutters.
7. Place 1 inch apart on ungreased cookie sheets.
8. Leave cookies plain for frosting, or brush with slightly beaten egg white and sprinkle with candy sprinkles or colored sugar.
9. Bake for 7 to 10 minutes or until light and golden brown; lift with spatula onto wire racks to cool.
10. Cool cookies completely before frosting.

Gingerbread Easter Cookies

The children always enjoy making and decorating these cookies. It is a great holiday tradition to start or share with your family.

Ingredients:

1⅓ c. brown sugar, firmly packed
⅓   c. butter, softened
1   egg
5   tsp. vanilla extract
2¾ c. molasses
5½ c. all-purpose flour
4   tsp. baking soda
2   tsp. salt
5½ tsp. ground cinnamon
3   tsp. ground ginger
    Vanilla Butter Cream Frosting (recipe page 129)

Directions:

1. Cream together brown sugar and butter.
2. Add egg, vanilla, and molasses; mix well.
3. Sift dry ingredients together and add to creamed mixture.
4. Cover and chill in refrigerator.
5. Preheat oven to 350 degrees F.
6. Roll dough ¼ inch thick on lightly floured surface.
7. Cut with gingerbread girl and gingerbread boy cutters.
8. Bake for about 8 to 10 minutes.
9. Lift with spatula onto wire racks to cool.
10. When cooled, frost with Vanilla Butter Cream Frosting.
11. Decorate as desired.

Just Good Cookies

Like the name says, these cookies are just plain good. The dough takes time and a lot of elbow grease, but there is not a better cookie anywhere. Try some today!

Ingredients:

3⅓ c. butter, softened
1⅓ c. sugar
4⅔ c. light brown sugar, firmly packed
8   eggs
4   tsp. baking soda
2   tsp. ground cinnamon
1   tsp. ground allspice
½   tsp. ground cloves
1   tsp. salt
1   Tbs. vanilla extract
1   Tbs. almond extract
½   c. grated orange peel
4   c. oatmeal
1⅓ c. chopped pecans
1½ c. golden raisins
12 oz. chocolate chips
12 oz. butterscotch chips
1   sm. pkg. coconut
6⅔ c. all-purpose flour

Directions:

1. Preheat oven to 350 degrees F.
2. Cream together butter and sugars until light and fluffy.
3. Beat in eggs one at a time until blended well.
4. Mix together soda, spices, and salt; add to creamed mixture.
5. Stir in vanilla and almond extracts, then add orange peel.
6. Mix in oatmeal, pecans, raisins, chips, and coconut, stirring well.
7. Add flour in small amounts until well blended.

8. Drop by spoonfuls onto cookie sheet, and bake 10 minutes or until lightly browned.
9. Lift with spatula onto wire racks to cool.

Molasses Crinkles

My mom used to make these when I was growing up, and I loved them. If you enjoy the taste of molasses and ginger, try these. They are delicious with a glass of ice cold milk.

Ingredients:

3 c. butter, softened
3¾ c. brown sugar, firmly packed
1½ c. dark molasses
4 eggs
9½ c. all-purpose flour
4 tsp. ground cinnamon
4 tsp. ground ginger
2 tsp. ground cloves
½ tsp. salt
2 tsp. baking soda

Directions:

1. Cream together butter, sugar, and molasses.
2. Add eggs one at a time, and blend well.
3. Sift together flour, spices, salt, and soda; add to wet mixture.
4. Cover and chill in refrigerator for 1 hour.
5. Preheat oven to 375 degrees F.
6. Shape into balls, place 2 inches apart on ungreased cookie sheets, and press flat with fork.
7. Sprinkle sugar on top.
8. Bake for 7 to 8 minutes.
9. Lift with spatula onto wire racks to cool.

Rainbow Cookies

These cookies are moist, mellow, and full of almond flavor. The recipe makes plenty of cookies to eat with some left over to freeze for those times you are in need of a quick snack for the family or company.

Ingredients:

- 8 oz. almond paste
- 1 c. butter, softened
- 1 c. sugar
- 4 eggs, separated
- 2 c. all-purpose flour
- 6 drops red food coloring
- 6 drops green food coloring
- ¼ c. seedless red raspberry jam
- ¼ c. apricot jam
- 1 c. semisweet chocolate chips, melted

Directions:

1. Preheat oven to 350 degrees F.
2. Line three 13 x 9 x 2-inch baking pans with parchment paper.
3. In large bowl break apart almond paste with fork; cream together with butter, sugar, and egg yolks.
4. When mixture is fluffy and smooth, add flour and stir until well blended.
5. In small bowl beat egg whites until soft peaks form.
6. Fold egg whites into dough, then divide dough into 3 equal portions.
7. Mix one portion with red food coloring and one with green food coloring.
8. Spread each portion into a prepared baking pan.
9. Bake 10 to 12 minutes, until lightly browned.
10. Turn each out of pan onto wire rack, remove parchment paper, and cool completely.
11. Place green layer onto piece of plastic wrap large enough to wrap all three layers.

160

12. Spread green layer with raspberry jam, and top with uncolored layer.
13. Spread with apricot jam, and top with pink layer.
14. Transfer layers to baking sheet, and enclose with plastic wrap.
15. Place heavy pan or cutting board on top of wrapped layers to compress.
16. Cover and chill in refrigerator 8 hours or overnight.
17. Remove plastic wrap; top with melted chocolate chips, then refrigerate 1 hour or until chocolate is firm.
18. Slice into small squares to serve.

Yields: 8 dozen.

Melting Dream Cookies

These are simple, smooth cookies that melt in your mouth.

Ingredients:

    1¼ c. all-purpose flour
    ¼ c. cornstarch
    ½ c. powdered sugar
    ¾ c. butter, softened

Directions:

1. Preheat oven to 350 degrees F.
2. Sift together flour, cornstarch, and powdered sugar.
3. Cut in butter until mixture begins to cling together.
4. Drop by spoonfuls onto cookie sheet about 2 inches apart; flatten with fork.
5. Bake for 20 to 25 minutes, until edges are golden brown.
6. Lift with spatula onto wire racks to cool.

Peanut Butter Cookies

Our entire family loves peanut butter cookies, so we make a lot of them.

Ingredients:

½ c. butter, softened
½ c. sugar
½ c. brown sugar, firmly packed
¾ c. peanut butter
2   eggs
½ tsp. vanilla extract
1¼ c. all-purpose flour
½ tsp. baking soda
½ tsp. baking powder
    additional sugar

Directions:

1. In mixing bowl cream together butter and sugars.
2. Add peanut butter, eggs, and vanilla; beat until smooth.
3. Combine flour, baking soda, and baking powder; add to creamed mixture and mix well.
4. For easier shaping, chill dough for 1 hour.
5. Preheat oven to 375 degrees F.
6. Shape dough into 1-inch balls; place 2 inches apart on ungreased baking sheets.
7. Flatten each ball by crisscrossing with tines of fork dipped in sugar.
8. Bake for 10 to 12 minutes or until bottoms are lightly browned and cookies are set.
9. Remove from oven; using spatula transfer to wire rack to cool.

Soft Ginger Cookies

These wonderful, soft cookies with a gentle spice flavor will become one of your family's favorites.

Ingredients:

1   c. sugar
¾   c. butter, softened
1   egg
¼   c. sorghum or molasses
2   tsp. baking soda
¼   tsp. salt
1   tsp. ground cinnamon
1   tsp. ground ginger
2   c. all-purpose flour

Directions:

1. Cream sugar and butter.
2. Add egg and molasses; beat well.
3. Sift together soda, salt, spices, and flour.
4. Add to creamed mixture and stir until well blended.
5. Cover and chill dough several hours or overnight in refrigerator.
6. Preheat oven to 375 degrees F.
7. Roll into small balls, dip in sugar, place on greased baking sheet, and flatten.
8. Bake for 15 to 18 minutes or until lightly browned.
9. Lift with spatula onto wire racks to cool.

Yields: 4 dozen.

Did You Know? . . . .

Did you know that the Easter lily, as well as some other types of lilies, are poisonous to cats?

Apple Tart Cookies

These cookies are made in the shape of small tarts and have an interesting and wholesome combination of ingredients you are sure to enjoy.

Ingredients:

    1½ c. butter, room temperature
    ⅓ c. peanut butter
    1½ c. brown sugar, firmly packed
    1½ c. sugar
    4   eggs
    2   tsp. almond extract
    2   c. all-purpose flour
    ½ c. whole-wheat flour
    4½ c. quick-cooking oatmeal
    ½ tsp. salt
    1   tsp. baking powder
    1   c. raisins
    1   c. shredded coconut
    1   c. chopped pecans
    1   pkg. soft dried apples, chopped

Directions:

1. Mix butter and peanut butter, then add sugars and cream well.
2. Put eggs in separate bowl, add almond extract, and whip slightly; add to creamed mixture.
3. In separate bowl mix together flours, oatmeal, salt, and baking powder.
4. Mix together dry and wet ingredients until well blended.
5. Stir in raisins, coconut, pecans, and chopped apples; dough will be stiff.
6. Chill mixture for 1 hour.
7. Preheat oven to 350 degrees F.
8. Shape cookies using ¼ measuring cup, packing cookie mixture in cup.

9. Drop out of cup onto greased cookie sheet, 2 inches apart.
10. Bake for 18 to 20 minutes, until light brown on top.
11. Remove from oven, let stand 5 minutes, then transfer to wire racks to cool.

Yields: About 4 dozen cookies.

Shortbread Cookies

My husband loves shortbread, and it is always his special request for his birthday.

Ingredients:

¾ c. butter, softened
¼ c. sugar
2 c. all-purpose flour

Directions:

1. In medium mixing bowl cream together butter and sugar; work flour in with your hands.
2. Chill dough in refrigerator for at least 2 hours.
3. Preheat oven to 350 degrees F.
4. Remove dough from refrigerator, and on very lightly floured surface, roll dough ⅓ to ½ inch thick, and cut into desired shapes.
5. Place on ungreased baking sheet about 2 inches apart.
6. Bake for 20 to 25 minutes only, as cookies should not brown on top.
7. Remove from oven and lift onto wire rack to cool.
8. Serve immediately or store in airtight container for up to 3 weeks.

Old-Fashioned Soft Sugar Cookies

Old-fashioned sugar cookies are always a special treat.

Ingredients for cookies:

    1½ c. powdered sugar
    1   c. butter, softened
    1   egg
    1   tsp. vanilla extract
    ½   tsp. almond extract
    3   c. all-purpose flour
    1   tsp. baking soda
    1   tsp. cream of tartar

Ingredients for frosting:

    ¼   c. butter, softened
    2   c. powdered sugar
    1   tsp. vanilla extract
    2   Tbs. milk

Directions for cookies:

1. Preheat oven to 375 degrees F.
2. Cream together sugar and butter.
3. Stir in egg, vanilla, and almond extract.
4. Add flour, soda, and cream of tartar; mix well.
5. Drop by spoonfuls onto baking sheet 2 inches apart.
6. Bake for 8 minutes or just until edges turn light brown.
7. Remove from oven, and lift with spatula onto wire racks to cool completely before frosting.

Directions for frosting:

1. Cream butter, powdered sugar, and vanilla.
2. Add milk a little at a time, until of a creamy consistency.
3. Spread over tops of cooled cookies and let sit until firm.
4. May store in airtight container up to 3 months.

Spritz Cookies

These spritz cookies are made with a press. They are a tradition in Europe on holidays, especially at tea time.

Ingredients:

½ c. butter, softened
3 oz. cream cheese, softened
⅓ c. sugar
1 egg yolk
1 tsp. lemon extract
1½ c. all-purpose flour
½ tsp. salt

Directions:

1. Preheat oven to 400 degrees F.
2. Cream butter, cream cheese, and sugar until light and fluffy.
3. Add egg yolk and extract, beating well.
4. Mix flour and salt together in bowl.
5. Add to creamed mixture in 3 additions, mixing well after each addition.
6. Fill cookie press, and make desired shapes on ungreased baking sheets about 1 inch apart.
7. Bake for 10 to 12 minutes or until lightly browned around edges.
8. Lift with spatula onto wire racks to cool.

Macadamia Nut Cookies

These excellent cookies are full of macadamia nuts that give them a crunchy texture and a delicious taste.

Ingredients:

- 2 c. all-purpose flour
- 1 tsp. baking soda
- ½ tsp. salt
- ¾ c. unsalted butter, softened
- 1 c. light brown sugar, firmly packed
- ½ c. sugar
- 2 eggs, room temperature
- 1 tsp. vanilla extract
- 14 oz. white chocolate, cut into ¼-in. chunks
- 1¾ c. coarsely chopped macadamia nuts

Directions:

1. Preheat oven to 300 degrees F.
2. Cover 2 cookie sheets with wax paper or foil; set aside.
3. Sift together flour, soda, and salt; set aside.
4. In large bowl beat butter at low speed of electric mixer until creamy; gradually add sugars and beat until light and fluffy.
5. Add eggs one at a time, beating well after each addition; stir in vanilla.
6. Add chocolate chunks and nuts, stirring well.
7. Use ¼ measuring cup to form cookies, packing dough into cup so it is even.
8. Drop on baking sheets, leaving 3 inches between cookies; flatten cookies slightly.
9. Bake for 20 to 25 minutes, until light brown on edges.
10. Cool 3 to 5 minutes in pan, then transfer to wire racks to finish cooling.

Easter Delights Cookbook
A Collection of Easter Recipes
Cookbook Delights Holiday Series-Book 4

Desserts

Table of Contents

Page

Did You Know? . . . .

Did you know that President Rutherford Hayes and his wife, Lucy, started the White House lawn egg rolling tradition in 1878? It had previously been held on the Capitol grounds.

Butterscotch Cheesecake with Chocolate Drizzle

It is hard to find a more delicious dessert with which to surprise your family or guests.

Ingredients for cheesecake:

1 graham cracker crust (recipe page 227)
3 pkg. cream cheese (8 oz. each), softened
½ c. sugar
2 Tbs. all-purpose flour
1⅔ c. butterscotch chips
2 Tbs. milk
4 eggs

Ingredients for chocolate drizzle:

½ c. semisweet chocolate chips
1 Tbs. shortening (no substitutes)

Directions for cheesecake:

1. Prepare graham cracker crust in spring form pan.
2. Preheat oven to 350 degrees F.
3. Beat cream cheese, sugar, and flour in large bowl on medium speed of mixer until smooth.
4. Place butterscotch chips and milk in small microwave-safe bowl; microwave on high for 1 minute, then stir.
5. Microwave on high an additional 15 seconds at a time just until chips are melted when stirred.
6. Cool, and then stir butterscotch mixture into cream cheese mixture.
7. Add eggs one at a time, blending well after each addition.
8. Pour mixture over prepared crust.
9. Bake for 40 to 45 minutes or until center is almost set; remove from oven to wire rack.
10. With knife, immediately loosen cake from side of pan.
11. Cool completely; remove side of pan.

Directions for chocolate drizzle:

1. Place chocolate chips and shortening (do not use butter, margarine, spread, or oil) in small microwave-safe bowl.
2. Microwave on high for 30 seconds; stir.
3. Microwave on high an additional 20 seconds or until chocolate is melted and mixture is smooth.
4. Drizzle over top of cheesecake; cover and refrigerate until ready to serve.

Berry Ice Box Dessert

My mom always made a version of this recipe for me when I was growing up. It is a great make-ahead dessert and keeps well in the freezer. Please note that this recipe does use raw eggs, which should be heated and cooled before using, as a safety precaution.

Ingredients:

1   box vanilla wafers, crushed
2   eggs
½   c. butter, softened
3   c. powdered sugar
6   c. huckleberries, strawberries, or blueberries
½   pt. cream, whipped, sweetened
1   c. ground nuts, divided

Directions:

1. Preheat oven to 350 degrees F.
2. Pat half the crushed wafers onto bottom of 12 x 8-inch baking pan, and bake for 8 to 10 minutes; cool.
3. Cream together eggs, butter, and powdered sugar.
4. Lightly stir together creamed mixture, berries, whipped cream, and ½ cup nuts.
5. Pour into pan, and sprinkle remaining crumbs and nuts over top; refrigerate overnight or freeze.
6. Remove from refrigerator, and let stand for a short time before serving.

Chocolate Cream Passover Torte

This is a nice dessert that is wonderful to serve not only at Passover but on other special occasions as well.

Ingredients for torte:

⅓ c. plus 1 Tbs. baking cocoa, divided
¼ c. boiling water
2 Tbs. butter, softened
1 tsp. vanilla extract
6 eggs, separated
¾ c. sugar, divided
⅓ c. finely ground toasted almonds

Ingredients for cocoa whipped cream:

1½ c. whipping cream, cold
⅓ c. sugar
3 Tbs. baking cocoa
¾ tsp. vanilla extract

Directions for torte:

1. Preheat oven to 350 degrees F.
2. To toast almonds: Spread ⅓ cup blanched slivered almonds in thin layer in shallow baking pan. Bake 8 to 10 minutes, stirring occasionally, until light golden brown. Cool completely, then grind in food processor. Set aside.
3. Line bottom of 15 x 10 x 1-inch jellyroll pan with parchment paper or line with foil extending slightly over sides; grease liner.
4. Stir together ⅓ cup cocoa and boiling water in small bowl until mixture is smooth.
5. Stir in butter and vanilla; cool.
6. Combine egg yolks and ½ cup sugar in large bowl; beat on medium speed of mixer until light and fluffy, about 5 minutes.

7. Mix chocolate mixture, ground almonds, and egg yolks together, blending well.
8. Beat egg whites in another large bowl until foamy.
9. Gradually add remaining ¼ cup sugar, beating until stiff peaks form.
10. Gently fold egg whites into chocolate mixture.
11. Pour batter into prepared pan.
12. Bake 18 to 20 minutes or until cake springs back when touched lightly in center.
13. Dust cake with remaining 1 tablespoon cocoa; cover with clean, dry towel.
14. Cool completely in pan on wire rack.
15. Cut cake into 4 equal pieces.
16. Remove paper or foil, then place one cake layer on plate; spread with whipped cream.
17. Repeat layering, ending with whipped cream.
18. Spread remaining whipped cream on all sides of assembled cake; garnish as desired.
19. Refrigerate until serving time. Cover and refrigerate any leftover dessert.

Directions for cocoa whipped cream:

1. Combine whipping cream, sugar, cocoa, and vanilla in large, cold bowl.
2. Beat with cold beaters until stiff.

Did You Know? . . . .

Did you know that PEEPS® chicks and bunnies come in 5 colors? Yellow chicks are the most popular, followed by pink, lavender, blue, and white.

Poteca

My mom always made Poteca for the holidays, and it is a long-time family tradition.

Ingredients for dough:

> 3-4 c. unsifted all-purpose flour, divided
> ¼ c. sugar
> 1 tsp. salt
> 1 pkg. active dry yeast
> ½ c. milk
> ½ c. water
> ¼ c. butter
> 1 egg, room temperature

Ingredients for pecan filling:

> ¼ c. butter, softened
> ½ c. brown sugar, firmly packed
> 1 egg
> 2 Tbs. milk
> 1 tsp. orange extract
> 2 c. finely chopped pecans

Directions for dough:

1. In large bowl thoroughly mix 1 cup flour, sugar, salt, and yeast; set aside.
2. Combine milk, water, and butter in saucepan.
3. Heat over low heat until liquids are very warm (120 to 130 degrees F). Butter does not need to melt.
4. Gradually add milk mixture and egg to dry ingredients, and beat 2 minutes at medium speed of electric mixer, scraping bowl occasionally.
5. Stir in enough additional flour to make soft dough.
6. Turn out onto lightly floured surface; knead until smooth and elastic, about 8 to 10 minutes.
7. Place in greased bowl, turning to grease top.
8. Cover; let rise in warm place, free from draft, until doubled in bulk, about 1½ hours.

9. Punch dough down; turn out on lightly floured surface.
10. Roll dough out to 20 x 5-inch rectangle.
11. Prepare filling and spread onto dough.
12. Starting at wide side of dough, roll up as for jellyroll.
13. Seal edges, then form into round coil shape on large, greased baking sheet.
14. Cover; let rise in warm place, free from draft, until doubled in bulk, about 1 hour.
15. Preheat oven to 325 degrees F.
16. Bake for 40 to 45 minutes or until done.
17. Remove from baking sheet and cool on wire rack.
18. May optionally drizzle powdered sugar glaze over top if you like sweeter bread.

Directions for pecan filling:

1. Mix together butter, brown sugar, and egg.
2. Stir in milk and orange extract.
3. Blend in pecans.

Sweetened Whipped Cream

There is nothing as rich and delicious as sweetened whipped cream.

Ingredients:

1   c. heavy cream
¼   c. sugar
1   tsp. vanilla extract

Directions:

1. Whip cream until almost stiff.
2. Add sugar and vanilla; beat until cream holds peaks.
3. Spread over top of cooled pie or dollop on bread pudding, gingerbread, cobblers, or other desserts.

Strawberry Scone Shortcake

Scones are always delicious. Add fresh strawberries and they are even better.

Ingredients for topping:

> fresh strawberries
> sugar
> whipping cream
> powdered sugar
> vanilla extract to taste

Ingredients for scones:

> 2   c. all-purpose flour
> 2½ tsp. baking powder
> ½   tsp. baking soda
> 1   tsp. salt
> ¼   c. sugar
> 1   egg
> 1   c. sour cream
> ½   tsp. vanilla extract

Directions for topping:

1. Early in the day, rinse, hull, and slice strawberries; add a little sugar to taste.
2. Refrigerate until serving time to allow juice to form.
3. Retain enough whole, perfect strawberries to use as garnish.
4. Just before serving, whip cream, sweeten with powdered sugar, and add vanilla.

Directions for scones and assembly:

1. Preheat oven to 375 degrees F.
2. In medium bowl combine flour, baking powder, baking soda, salt, and sugar.

3. In small bowl beat egg with whisk, then whisk in sour cream and vanilla.
4. Make well in dry ingredients, and add egg mixture all at once; stir to make soft dough.
5. Turn out onto floured surface, and knead 10 times.
6. Separate dough in half, and pat each half into circle ½ to ¾ inch thick and 6 inches wide.
7. Cut each circle into 6 wedges; place on ungreased baking sheet, and bake for 15 minutes.
8. To assemble each serving, turn scone on side and cut in half, placing bottom half on plate.
9. Spoon strawberries and some juice over top.
10. Spoon whipped cream over top of strawberries, then top with top of scone.
11. Garnish with small spoonful of whipped cream and a whole strawberry.

Strawberry Surprise

This light dessert is especially flavorful and just right to top off a holiday dinner.

Ingredients:

1   lb. fresh strawberries, washed
3   oz. brandy
5   oz. heavy whipping cream
½   tsp. vanilla extract

Directions:

1. Hull strawberries and place in bowl.
2. Pour brandy over strawberries, and put in refrigerator for 1 hour.
3. Divide strawberries among 4 individual serving glasses.
4. Whip cream and vanilla until stiff; spoon over strawberries, and serve.

Apple Strudel

I have fond memories of my mom making homemade apple strudel when I was young. This is one of the easier recipes and definitely worth making. It is great served warm right out of the oven with vanilla ice cream and dusted with fresh-ground cinnamon.

Ingredients:

2 c. all-purpose flour
1 tsp. salt
⅓ lb. plus 2 Tbs. butter, melted, divided
1 Tbs. cooking oil
2 eggs
¼ c. warm water
12 apples, chopped or finely grated
1 c. sugar
1½ tsp. ground cinnamon (optional)

Directions:

1. Sift flour into bowl and form well.
2. Mix together salt, 2 tablespoons melted butter, oil, eggs, and warm water.
3. Pour into flour well and work in gradually.
4. After thorough mixing, cover with warm, wet cloth; let stand about 1 hour.
5. Preheat oven to 400 degrees F.
6. Turn dough out onto floured surface, and roll very thin, until it covers a circle 28 to 30 inches in diameter.
7. Brush about half the ⅓ pound melted butter onto thin, stretched dough.
8. Sprinkle on apples, sugar, cinnamon (if desired), and remaining butter.
9. Roll tightly, tucking in corners as you roll.
10. Shape roll into horseshoe shape, and place seam side down in lightly greased large pan.

11. Bake for 10 minutes, then reduce oven to 350 degrees, and bake for 50 minutes or until done.
12. Remove from oven, and slide out onto wire rack to cool.
13. Sprinkle with powdered sugar or drizzle with frosting after cooling to lukewarm.

Cheesecake

This is an easy-to-make version of cheesecake that is very tasty. You may use your favorite fruit to complete this delicious dessert.

Ingredients:

1   graham cracker crust (recipe page 227)
2   pkg. cream cheese (8 oz. each), softened
¾   c. sugar
¼   tsp. vanilla extract
2   eggs
1½ c. fruit of choice, cut into small bits, divided

Directions:

1. Prepare graham cracker crust in 9-inch pie plate.
2. Preheat oven to 350 degrees F.
3. Mix cream cheese, sugar, and vanilla until smooth and creamy.
4. Add eggs and mix well; pour into pie crust.
5. Spoon half of fruit on top; gently swirl with knife.
6. Bake for 40 minutes or until center is set.
7. Remove from oven and cool to room temperature, then refrigerate.
8. When ready to serve, top with remaining fruit.

Black Bottom Butterscotch Cream Pie

This pie takes some extra time to make, but it is well worth it.

Ingredients for shell:

1 c. pecans
2 Tbs. sugar
1¼ c. all-purpose flour
6 Tbs. cold unsalted butter, cut into bits
½ tsp. salt
3 Tbs. ice water
6 oz. fine quality bittersweet chocolate
¼ c. heavy cream
   uncooked rice for weighting crust

Ingredients for filling:

1 Tbs. bourbon
2 Tbs. water
1 env. unflavored gelatin (about 1 Tbs.)
1 c. dark brown sugar, firmly packed
1 c. milk
¾ tsp. salt
2 Tbs. unsalted butter
3 lg. egg yolks
½ tsp. vanilla extract
¾ c. heavy cream
   freshly grated nutmeg to taste

Ingredients for decoration:

¼ c. sugar
10 pecan halves
1 c. heavy cream

Directions for shell:

1. In food processor coarsely grind pecans with sugar, and then transfer mixture to a bowl.
2. In food processor blend together flour, butter, and salt until mixture resembles meal; add flour mixture to pecan mixture.
3. Add ice water, tossing mixture until water is incorporated; press onto bottom and up side of 9-inch pie plate, crimping edge decoratively.
4. Chill shell for 1 hour, then prick all over with fork, and line with foil.
5. Preheat oven to 425 degrees F.
6. Fill foil with rice; bake in lower third of oven for 10 minutes, then remove foil and rice carefully.
7. Reduce oven to 375 degrees F., and bake for 12 to 15 minutes more or until golden brown; cool on rack.
8. In small metal bowl set over pan of barely simmering water, melt chocolate with cream, stirring until mixture is smooth.
9. Spread mixture in bottom and halfway up side of the shell; let cool then chill shell.

Directions for filling:

1. Make filling while shell is chilling.
2. In large metal bowl combine bourbon and water; sprinkle gelatin over liquid, and let it soften.
3. In saucepan heat brown sugar, milk, and salt over moderate heat, stirring, until mixture is hot and sugar is dissolved; whisk in butter. (Mixture will appear slightly curdled.)
4. In bowl whisk egg yolks; add hot milk mixture in a stream, whisking, then pour mixture back into pan.
5. Cook custard over moderately low heat, whisking constantly, until thickened and registers 160 degrees F. on a candy thermometer.

6. Add to gelatin mixture; stir in vanilla and nutmeg.
7. Set in bowl of ice water, and stir mixture until it is cold and consistency of raw egg whites, then remove bowl from ice water.
8. In another bowl with electric mixer, beat cream until it holds stiff peaks; fold into custard mixture gently but thoroughly, and pour filling into chilled shell.
9. Chill pie for 6 hours or overnight.

Directions for decoration:

1. In very small skillet or saucepan, cook sugar over moderate heat, undisturbed, until it begins to melt, then cook, stirring with fork, until it is melted completely and turns a golden caramel; reduce heat to low.
2. Working quickly, add pecans, turning to coat thoroughly with caramel.
3. With fork transfer them one at a time to piece of foil to cool.
4. In chilled bowl with chilled beaters, beat cream until it holds stiff peaks.
5. Drop by heaping tablespoons around edge of pie.
6. Arrange a caramelized pecan in center of each dollop.

Yields: 6 to 8 servings.

Easter Almond Pudding

Almonds add great flavor to this Easter pudding that originated in Europe.

Ingredients:

1   oz. unsalted butter
1   c. milk
1   c. heavy cream
1   piece cinnamon stick
1   lemon rind, grated

3	oz. superfine sugar
4	oz. almonds, ground
½	tsp. ground nutmeg
1	pinch salt
6	oz. fine bread crumbs
4	oz. almond cookies, crushed (plain or shortbread)
4	eggs, slightly beaten
2	Tbs. candied peel
2	Tbs. currants or raisins

Directions:

1. Preheat oven to 375 degrees F.
2. Lightly butter glass casserole dish and set aside.
3. In saucepan over medium heat, bring milk and cream to a boil.
4. Reduce heat and add cinnamon, lemon rind, and sugar; stir well and simmer for about 10 minutes.
5. Pour milk mixture through sieve to remove rind and cinnamon stick.
6. Stir in ground almonds and blend well.
7. Leave mixture to simmer a bit, then add nutmeg and salt.
8. Place bread crumbs and crushed almond cookies in mixing bowl.
9. Combine a few tablespoons of milk mixture with slightly beaten eggs, then add all of the mixture to bread crumbs along with candied peel and currants or raisins; blend well.
10. Pour into the prepared casserole dish, and bake for about 45 minutes.
11. Remove from oven and cool before serving with cream.
12. Refrigerate remaining pudding.

Did You Know? . . . .

Did you know that the famous sunrise service on Mount Rubidoux in California was first held in 1909?

Tiramisu

Tiramisu is one of our favorite family dessert recipes. Try this delicious recipe and enjoy.

Ingredients:

5   egg yolks
½   c. plus 2 Tbs. sugar, divided
¼   c. water
6   oz. mascarpone cheese
4   Tbs. sweet Marsala wine, divided
1¼ c. heavy whipping cream, whipped
2   c. espresso or strong coffee
2   oz. dark rum
24 French-style ladyfingers
2   Tbs. powdered sweetened cocoa mix
4   Tbs. grated semisweet chocolate

Directions:

1. Using electric mixer, beat egg yolks and ½ cup sugar until light, about 5 minutes.
2. Whisk in water, transfer to double boiler set over gently simmering water, and whisk about 7 minutes, until thickened; let cool.
3. With mixer on medium speed, add mascarpone cheese and 2 tablespoons Marsala wine to egg mixture, whipping until smooth, and then fold in whipped cream.
4. To prepare espresso mixture, combine espresso, remaining 2 tablespoons Marsala, dark rum, and remaining 2 tablespoons sugar.
5. Heat to 140 degrees F., then place in refrigerator to cool completely.
6. Remove from refrigerator and quickly dip ladyfingers in espresso mixture one at a time, placing a layer on bottom of sided glass serving dish.

7. Divide creamed filling in half, and top ladyfinger layer with half of cream mixture.
8. Add another layer of dipped ladyfingers, topping with a second layer of cream mixture.
9. Sift cocoa lightly over top and sprinkle with grated chocolate.
10. Cover and refrigerate overnight.
11. Can be frozen for up to 2 weeks; let defrost in refrigerator for 24 hours before serving.

Yields: 8 servings.

Cantaloupe Sherbet

This makes a light and refreshing dessert after a large meal. It is also a satisfying snack on a hot afternoon.

Ingredients:

1	sm. cantaloupe, seeded, peeled, cubed
2	Tbs. lemon juice
3	c. half-and-half
½	c. superfine sugar
¼	c. honey
1	tsp. pure vanilla extract

Directions:

1. Place melon and lemon juice in blender or food processor; purée until smooth.
2. Pour into large bowl; whisk in half-and-half, sugar, honey, and vanilla extract, stirring until sugar dissolves.
3. Place mixture in ice cream machine, and freeze according to manufacturer's directions.

Two-Tone Dessert

My mom liked to make this chocolate dish that we all enjoyed. It is a delicious combination of chocolate and whipped cream.

Ingredients:

1   c. all-purpose flour
½ c. butter, softened
½ c. chopped nuts
8   oz. cream cheese, softened
1   c. powdered sugar
1   lg. container prepared whipped cream
2   sm. pkg. instant chocolate pudding
2½ c. milk
    toasted coconut

Directions:

1. Preheat oven to 350 degrees F.
2. Spray 13 x 9 x 2-inch pan with nonstick spray.
3. Mix flour, butter, and nuts together, and then press into bottom of pan.
4. Bake for 10 to 15 minutes.
5. Remove from oven and set aside to cool.
6. Add powdered sugar to cream cheese, and beat until light and fluffy.
7. Add about ½ the whipped cream to cream cheese mixture, and then spread over cooled crust.
8. In mixing bowl mix milk with pudding, beating until thick; spread over whipped cream mixture.
9. Spread remaining whipped cream over top of pudding mixture; spread toasted coconut over top of whipped cream.
10. Refrigerate until ready to serve. Keeps well for several days.

Dressings, Sauces, and Condiments

Table of Contents

Did You Know? . . . .

Did you know that in the early 1950s, it took 27 hours to make one PEEPS® chick. Today it takes six minutes!

Apricot Rosemary Salsa

This salsa is great served with pork or fowl. Try it this Easter for a twist on the traditional meal.

Ingredients:

- ½   c. peaches or apricots, pitted, peeled, chopped
- ¼   c. avocado, pitted, peeled, chopped
- ¼   c. tomato, chopped
- ½   tsp. finely grated lime or lemon peel
- 2   Tbs. lime or lemon juice
- 1   Tbs. green onion, thinly sliced
- 1   tsp. snipped fresh rosemary (or ½ tsp. dried)

Directions:

1. In small bowl stir together peaches or apricots, avocado, tomato, citrus peel, citrus juice, green onion, and rosemary.
2. Cover and chill in refrigerator for up to 24 hours to meld flavors before serving.

Yields: 1 cup.

Green Goddess Dressing

This is one of those dressings that will add to, as well as enhance, the taste of any salad.

Ingredients:

- 1   c. mayonnaise
- ½   c. sour cream
- 3   Tbs. tarragon vinegar
- 1   Tbs. lemon juice

⅓ c. finely chopped parsley
3 Tbs. finely minced onion
3 Tbs. mashed anchovy fillets
1 Tbs. chopped capers
1 clove garlic, minced
¼ tsp. salt
¼ tsp. pepper

Directions:

1. Combine mayonnaise, sour cream, vinegar, and lemon juice.
2. Fold in parsley, onion, mashed anchovy, capers, and garlic, blending well.
3. Add salt and pepper.
4. Place in covered container, and refrigerate for 3 to 4 hours before using.
5. May be kept in refrigerator in unopened, airtight container for up to 2 weeks.

Yields: About 2 cups.

Russian Dressing

Try this Russian dressing for a zingy salad dressing.

Ingredients:

1 c. mayonnaise
¼ c. ketchup
1 Tbs. horseradish
1 tsp. grated onion

Directions:

1. Combine ingredients, shake well, and serve.

Ranch Dressing

This ranch dressing has higher protein content, and it is still very tasty.

Ingredients:

- 2 c. low-fat cottage cheese
- ½ c. low-fat yogurt, drained
- 2 sm. cloves garlic, minced
- 1 tsp. dried oregano
- 1 tsp. dried thyme
- 2 tsp. chopped fresh parsley
- ½ c. buttermilk
- 2 Tbs. lemon juice
- 1 Tbs. red wine vinegar
  freshly ground white pepper to taste

Directions:

1. Using blender with steel blade, combine first 7 ingredients until smooth.
2. Stir in lemon juice, vinegar, and white pepper.
3. Blend all ingredients until creamy and smooth.
4. Place in airtight container in refrigerator until ready to use.

Yields: Approximately 2½ cups.

Blue Cheese Oil and Vinegar Salad Dressing

This blue cheese vinaigrette is wonderful over mixed greens.

Ingredients:

- 1 c. salad oil
- 3 Tbs. red wine vinegar
- 1 tsp. salt
- ¼ tsp. pepper
- ¼ tsp. paprika
- 1 clove garlic, minced

½ tsp. celery salt
1 Tbs. lemon juice
1 Tbs. Worcestershire sauce
½ c. blue cheese, crumbled

Directions:

1. Mix together all ingredients except blue cheese, blending well.
2. Gradually fold in crumbled blue cheese.
3. Chill, covered, for at least 6 hours to mellow flavors.
4. May be kept in unopened airtight container in refrigerator for up to 3 months.

Yields: 1¾ cups.

Creamy Pesto Sauce

Quick and easy pesto is a great change from red sauce over your favorite pasta. My family really enjoys this tasty pesto sauce.

Ingredients:

3   c. fresh basil leaves
1½ c. chopped walnuts
4   cloves garlic, peeled
⅓   c. freshly grated Parmesan cheese
1   c. olive oil
     salt and pepper to taste

Directions:

1. In food processor blend together basil leaves, nuts, garlic, and cheese.
2. Pour in oil slowly while still mixing.
3. Stir in salt and pepper.
4. Blend all ingredients well before serving.
5. May be kept in refrigerator in unopened airtight container for up to 2 weeks.

Yields: 2 cups.

Papaya Seed Dressing

This is one of our family's favorite recipes, and it is great served over sliced fresh papaya and avocado salad. Try adding shrimp or other fresh seafood to your salad for a change of pace.

Ingredients:

- 1 c. olive oil
- ½ c. chopped onion
- ¼ c. papaya seeds, reserve papaya for slices
- 1 c. balsamic vinegar
- ⅓ c. sugar
- ¼ tsp. dry mustard
- 4 tsp. salt

Directions:

1. Combine oil, onion, papaya seeds, and vinegar in blender; blend until seeds look like ground pepper.
2. Add sugar, mustard, and salt to taste, blending well, then refrigerate dressing.
3. Right before serving, place on individual plates any greens such as iceberg lettuce, romaine lettuce, or mixed greens.
4. Top with celery, cucumbers, avocado, and papaya slices.
5. Serve dressing in bowl on the side.

Yields: About 3 cups.

Did You Know? . . . .

Did you know that the amount of PEEPS® chicks and bunnies eaten at Easter could more than circle Earth's circumference?

Rhubarb and Raisin Chutney

Rhubarb adds a nice spring flavor to your classic raisin chutney.

Ingredients:

- 3   Tbs. vegetable oil
- 1   c. golden raisins
- ½   c. hot water
- 3   Tbs. red wine vinegar
- ⅛   tsp. ground cloves
- ½   c. sugar
- 1   lb. rhubarb, trimmed, cut into ½-in. pieces
-     salt and pepper

Directions:

1. In medium saucepan combine oil, raisins, hot water, vinegar, cloves, and sugar; let stand 15 minutes.
2. Bring mixture to a boil, stirring constantly.
3. Add rhubarb, cover, and cook at slow boil for 5 minutes.
4. Stir mixture and continue cooking, uncovered, 3 to 5 minutes more or until rhubarb is just tender.
5. Season to taste with salt and pepper.
6. May be made 1 week in advance, kept in airtight container, and chilled in refrigerator until ready to serve.
7. Serve warm or at room temperature.

Did You Know? . . . .

Did you know that the celebrated Fabergé workshops created exquisite jeweled Easter eggs for the Russian Imperial Court?

Tomato Alfredo Sauce

My daughter Kelsey enjoys tomato Alfredo on her pasta. This version uses sour cream instead of the usual whipping cream.

Ingredients:

    1   c. sour cream
    ¾   c. grated Parmesan cheese
    1   can diced tomatoes (14 oz.)
        salt and pepper

Directions:

1. Mix together sour cream, Parmesan cheese, diced tomatoes, and salt and pepper to taste in saucepan, and bring to simmer.
2. Simmer over low heat 5 minutes to blend flavors.
3. When ready to serve, pour over your favorite pasta.

Yields: About 2½ cups.

Thousand Island Dressing

Try this homemade version of the traditional Thousand Island dressing.

Ingredients:

    ½   c. mayonnaise
    2   Tbs. ketchup
    1   Tbs. white vinegar
    2   tsp. sugar
    2   tsp. dill pickle relish
    1   tsp. finely minced white onion
    ⅛   tsp. salt
    1   dash black pepper

Directions:

1. Combine mayonnaise, ketchup, vinegar, and sugar in small bowl; stir well.
2. Add relish and onion; season with salt and black pepper to taste, blending well.
3. Place dressing in covered container and refrigerate for several hours, stirring occasionally, to dissolve sugar and blend flavors.
4. May be kept in unopened airtight container for up to 2 weeks in refrigerator.

Yields: ¾ cup.

Balsamic Vinaigrette Dressing

My daughter Marissa loves balsamic vinegar, and this makes a tasty dressing.

Ingredients:

½ c. balsamic vinegar
1 Tbs. soy sauce
2 Tbs. honey
2 cloves garlic, minced
½ c. extra-virgin olive oil
crushed dried red pepper to taste

Directions:

1. In medium bowl or food processor, whisk together balsamic vinegar, soy sauce, honey, garlic, and red pepper.
2. Add olive oil in thin stream, whisking until emulsified.
3. Refrigerate until ready to use.

Chokecherry Sauce

If you have access to chokecherries, this recipe makes a delicious sauce to use on pancakes.

Ingredients:

1½ c. chokecherries
¾ c. cold water
1   box cherry gelatin (3 oz.)
2   Tbs. fresh orange juice
2   Tbs. unsalted butter
½   tsp. honey

Directions:

1. Place chokecherries in medium saucepan, and pour water on top.
2. Bring to a boil, and then reduce heat to low; cover and simmer about 10 minutes.
3. Reduce heat to lowest setting, and stir in dry gelatin, orange juice, butter, and honey, mixing until blended well and butter has melted.
4. Serve hot over pancakes.

Creamy Vinaigrette

Some people are hesitant to try a creamy version of vinaigrette, but it is really good.

Ingredients:

¼   c. rice wine vinegar
2   Tbs. mayonnaise
1   lg. clove garlic, minced
⅔   c. olive oil
    salt and pepper

Directions:

1. Measure vinegar and mayonnaise into medium bowl.
2. With small whisk, stir in garlic and a big pinch of salt and pepper.
3. Pouring slowly, whisk oil into mixture; add first in droplets then in slow, steady stream to make emulsified vinaigrette as you whisk.
4. Place in airtight shaker container in refrigerator until ready to use.

Yields: About 1 cup.

Alfredo Sauce

My daughter loves Alfredo Sauce, and it is very easy to make. Kelsey likes it mixed half and half with marinara sauce, which is also excellent.

Ingredients:

4	Tbs. butter
8	oz. heavy whipping cream
1	pinch salt
1	pinch ground nutmeg
⅓	c. grated Parmesan cheese
⅓	c. grated Romano cheese
2	egg yolks, beaten
	grated Parmesan cheese

Directions:

1. Melt butter in saucepan over medium heat.
2. Add heavy cream, stirring constantly.
3. Stir in salt, nutmeg, Parmesan cheese, and Romano cheese.
4. Stir constantly until melted, and then mix in egg yolks.
5. Simmer over medium-low heat for 3 to 5 minutes.
6. Garnish with additional grated Parmesan cheese.

Raisin Chutney

Raisin chutney is great when added as a side dish to your Easter meal. It is also very good served with your Easter ham.

Ingredients:

- 1   c. raisins
- 1   Tbs. freshly chopped ginger
- ½   tsp. cayenne
- 4   Tbs. water
- ½   lemon, juiced
- ½   tsp. salt or to taste

Directions:

1. Combine raisins, ginger, and cayenne in blender to form coarse paste.
2. Add water, lemon juice, and salt to taste; blend well.
3. Place in refrigerator in covered container until ready to use.
4. Will keep for about 2 weeks in airtight container in refrigerator.

Yields: About 1 cup.

Did You Know? . . . .

Did you know that in the North of England at Easter time, a traditional game called "egg dumping" or "egg jarping" is played? Hard-boiled pace eggs are distributed, and each player hits the other player's egg with their own. The winner is the holder of the last intact egg.

Easter Delights Cookbook
A Collection of Easter Recipes
Cookbook Delights Holiday Series-Book 4

Jams, Jellies, and Syrups

Table of Contents

Page

Did You Know? . . . .

Did you know that the oldest tradition is to use dyed and painted chicken eggs for Easter eggs? A modern custom is to substitute chocolate eggs or plastic eggs filled with confectionery such as jellybeans.

A Basic Guide for Canning Jams, Jellies and Syrups

1. Wash jars in hot, soapy water inside and out with brush or soft cloth.
2. Run your finger around rim of each jar, discarding any with cracks or chips.
3. Rinse well in clean, clear, hot water, using tongs to avoid burns to hands or fingers.
4. Place upside down on clean cloth to drain well.
5. Place lids in boiling water for 2 minutes to sterilize and keep hot until placing on rim of jar.
6. Immediately prior to filling each jar, immerse in very hot water with tongs to heat jar (avoids breakage of jar with hot liquid).
7. Fill jar to within 1 inch of top of rim or to level recommended in recipe.
8. Wipe rim with clean damp cloth to remove any particles of food, and check again for any chips or cracks.
9. With tongs, place lid from hot bath directly onto rim of jar.
10. Using gloves, cloth, or holders, tighten lid firmly onto jar with ring or use single formed lid in place of ring to cover inner lid. Do not tighten down too hard as it may impede sealing.
11. Place on protected surface to cool, taking care to not disturb lid and ring. A slight indentation of lid will be apparent when sealed.
12. Leave overnight until thoroughly cooled.
13. When cooled, wipe jars with damp cloth and then label and date each.
14. Store upright on shelf in cool, dark place.

Chokecherry Jelly

Chokecherry jelly, with its rich, distinctive flavor, is very refreshing and tastes great on your favorite toast or English muffin.

Ingredients:

1   gal. chokecherries
1   qt. water
1   Tbs. lemon juice
2   Tbs. powdered pectin
    sugar (1¼ c. per cup prepared juice)

Directions:

1. Wash chokecherries.
2. In large stainless steel pan, combine chokecherries with water and bring to a boil.
3. Simmer about 25 minutes or until chokecherries are soft; cool to lukewarm.
4. Strain through sieve, pressing gently so some pulp is mixed with juice. (The pulp gives body to syrup.)
5. Measure juice before returning to pan.
6. Add lemon juice and pectin to chokecherry juice, and stir well; heat to a rolling boil and boil 1 minute.
7. Add sugar; return to rolling boil, and boil 1 minute.
8. Remove from heat and skim; pour into sterilized jars, and process following canning directions on page 200.

Did You Know? . . . .

Did you know that in Medieval Europe, churchgoers would take a walk after Easter Mass, led by a crucifix or the Easter candle?

Rhubarb Berry Freezer Jam

This is a delightful jam. You may substitute frozen fruit for the fresh if necessary.

Ingredients:

8   c. chopped fresh rhubarb
3   c. sugar
4   c. fresh blueberries
1   pkg. strawberry-flavored gelatin (3 oz.)
1   pkg. raspberry-flavored gelatin (3 oz.)

Directions:

1. Combine rhubarb, sugar, and blueberries in large pot.
2. Bring to rolling boil over medium-high heat, and boil for 10 minutes longer.
3. Stir in dry gelatin until dissolved.
4. Transfer to sterile freezer tubs and cool.
5. Cover and refrigerate, or freeze any jam you do not intend to use right away.

Raspberry Jalapeño Jelly

This refreshing jelly is great as a glaze for roasted pork, leg of lamb, or even a ham.

Ingredients:

1   c. raspberries, fresh or frozen
½   c. chopped green bell pepper
¼   c. chopped jalapeño pepper
3   c. sugar
¾   c. apple cider vinegar
6   oz. liquid pectin
1   sprig fresh mint

Directions:

1. In large cooking pot combine raspberries, bell pepper, jalapeño pepper, sugar, and cider vinegar.
2. Bring to a boil over medium-high heat, and boil rapidly for 1 minute.
3. Remove from heat and let stand for 5 minutes.
4. Run mixture through strainer to remove bits of peppers, then stir in liquid pectin and boil for another minute.
5. Remove from heat and skim; pour into sterilized jars, and process following canning directions on page 200.

Mint Jelly

Mint jelly is both refreshing and a perfect addition to your Easter table. It is great with your Easter lamb.

Ingredients:

½ c. vinegar
1 c. water
½ c. mint leaves
3½ c. sugar
½ c. liquid pectin
   green food coloring

Directions:

1. In medium pan combine vinegar, water, mint leaves, and enough coloring to give tint desired.
2. Add sugar, stir, and bring to a boil.
3. Add pectin at once, stirring constantly, and bring again to a full boil for 1 minute.
4. Strain off mint leaves and skim if necessary.
5. Pour into sterilized jars, and process following canning directions on page 200.

Blackberry Jam

This makes a delicious blackberry jam.

Ingredients:

5½ c. blackberries, fresh or frozen
1   pkg. powdered fruit pectin
7   c. sugar

Directions:

1. Rinse and remove stems and hulls from berries; thoroughly crush, removing seeds from half the berries by sieving.
2. Stir fruit pectin into prepared berries.
3. In nonreactive 6- to 8-quart pan, bring fruit and pectin mixture to a full boil, stirring constantly.
4. When berry mixture has come to a full boil, remove from heat, and stir in sugar completely.
5. Return to heat, and return to full rolling boil for 1 minute, stirring constantly, then remove from heat.
6. Skim, pour into sterilized jars, and process following canning directions on page 200.

Yields: Approximately 8 cups.

Carrot Raspberry Preserves

Carrots and raspberries in combination make interesting preserves, and they are loaded with vitamins.

Ingredients:

2   lb. carrots, peeled, sliced
2   lb. raspberries
2   lb. sugar
6   pkg. powdered fruit pectin

Directions:

1. Place carrots in pot with enough water to cover.
2. Bring to a boil, cover, and cook until tender.

3. Drain, reserving ½ cup liquid; purée carrots and reserved liquid, then transfer to large pot.
4. Add raspberries, sugar, and pectin; stir until sugar is dissolved.
5. Bring to a slow boil and simmer gently for 20 minutes, stirring occasionally to prevent burning.
6. Remove from heat, skim foam, pour into sterilized jars, and process following canning directions on page 200.

Tomato Jam

This jam is good with meat dishes, and it is a flavorful, colorful addition to your Easter menu.

Ingredients:

10 lb. ripe red tomatoes
4 lb. sugar
4 lemons
8 cinnamon sticks, broken into 1 x ¼-in. bits

Directions:

1. Peel tomatoes and core stem end.
2. Place peeled tomatoes in 2-gallon, nonreactive stock pot. (Do not use aluminum.)
3. Boil peeled tomatoes; keep stirring and ladling off thin tomato juice until what remains is semi thick. Continue this process until most of the thin liquid is removed.
4. While continuing to stir, add sugar equal to ⅔ the volume of the purée.
5. Halve lemons and slice ¼ inch thick; add to pan along with cinnamon bits.
6. Stir mixture periodically to keep it from sticking to bottom of pot; cook until jam reaches consistency desired, then pour into sterile jars.
7. Process following canning directions on page 200.

Gooseberry Jelly

My husband loves gooseberries, and this makes an excellent Easter jelly.

Ingredients:

    3   lb. green gooseberries
    3   lb. sugar
    1   pkg. pectin

Directions:

1. Wash gooseberries; remove stems and blossom ends.
2. Cover with water; cook slowly until soft.
3. Drain through jelly bag.
4. Combine sugar and juice in equal proportions, stir well and add pectin.
5. Bring to a boil, and then boil rapidly until jelly sheets from spoon.
6. Remove from heat and skim; pour into sterilized jars, and process following canning directions on page 200.

Strawberry Kiwi Jam

This jam has a refreshingly tropical flavor with the addition of kiwis.

Ingredients:

    2¾ c. strawberries, crushed
    1¼ c. kiwifruit, peeled, chopped
    3¼ c. sugar
    1   pkg. powdered pectin

Directions:

1. Measure prepared fruits into large cooking pot, and bring to a boil.
2. Stir in sugar, then pectin; return to a boil, and boil for 1 minute longer.
3. Remove from heat and skim; pour into sterilized jars, and process following canning directions on page 200.

Sweet Onion Jelly

This onion jelly is great with beef, chicken, or pork. Try using it on your favorite meat sandwich.

Ingredients:

3   c. chopped sweet onions
¾   c. cider vinegar
3   c. sugar
1   tsp. crushed red pepper flakes
1   pkg. powdered fruit pectin

Directions:

1. Purée onion and vinegar in blender until smooth.
2. Pour into large cooking pot.
3. Add sugar and red pepper flakes; bring to a boil over medium-high heat.
4. Boil 5 minutes then add powdered pectin, stirring to combine; return to a hard boil and boil for 1 minute.
5. Remove from heat and skim; pour into sterilized jars, and process following canning directions on page 200.

Yields: 3½ cups.

Grape Jelly

Grape juice is a family favorite, and so is grape jelly. The purple color is perfect for Easter.

Ingredients:

3½ lb. Concord grapes
½ c. water
3 c. sugar

Directions:

1. To prepare juice select ¼ firm ripe and ¾ fully ripe grapes.
2. Wash and stem grapes; place in large cooking pot.
3. Crush grapes and add water; cover, and bring to a boil over high heat, stirring constantly.
4. Reduce heat; simmer for 10 minutes.
5. Strain juice through damp jelly bag or several layers of cheesecloth.
6. To prevent formation of tartrate crystals in jelly, let juice stand in cool place 12 to 24 hours, then strain again to remove crystals.
7. Place juice back into large cooking pot; add sugar, stirring until dissolved.
8. Boil over high heat, stirring constantly to 220 degrees F. or until jelly mixture sheets from spoon.
9. Remove from heat and skim; pour into sterilized jars, and process following canning directions on page 200.

Did You Know? . . . .

Did you know that Easter cards arrived in Victorian England when a stationer added a greeting to a drawing of a rabbit?

Huckleberry Jelly

For those of you who prefer clear jelly over jam, try this recipe. It will add another great purple color for your Easter dinner.

Ingredients:

    5½ c. huckleberry juice (directions follow)
    2   pkg. powdered fruit pectin
    2   Tbs. lemon juice
    8   c. sugar
    ½   tsp. almond extract

Directions:

1. To prepare huckleberry juice, crush 7 cups of huckleberries.
2. Add 1 cup water, and cook mixture in saucepan over low to moderate heat until soft.
3. Cool to room temperature, then squeeze through double thickness of cheesecloth; discard residue.
4. Combine huckleberry juice, pectin, and lemon juice in kettle.
5. Bring to rolling boil over medium-high heat, stirring constantly.
6. Add sugar all at once; continue stirring until mixture returns to a full boil.
7. Boil for 1 minute; remove from heat.
8. Stir in almond extract, then skim off foam; pour into sterilized jars, and process following canning directions on page 200.

Did You Know? . . . .

Did you know that in parts of Germany and Austria, green eggs are used on Maundy Thursday (Holy Thursday)?

Cranberry Jelly

Cranberry jelly is a refreshing and colorful addition to your Easter table.

Ingredients:

2   c. fresh cranberries
1   c. concentrated apple juice
¼   c. lemon juice
3   oz. liquid pectin
5   Tbs. glycerin
1   Tbs. unflavored gelatin

Directions:

1. Wash and pick over cranberries, discarding any that are soft.
2. Place in deep saucepan, and add fruit juices.
3. Cover and simmer for about 20 minutes, until fruit is soft.
4. Mash to break up any berries left whole, then strain through food mill or sieve to remove seeds.
5. Return to saucepan and heat to boiling.
6. Set pan off burner and add pectin, glycerin, and gelatin, stirring well; return to burner and boil for 1 minute.
7. Remove from heat and skim; pour into sterilized jars, and process following canning directions on page 200.

Did You Know? . . . .

Did you know that boiling hard-cooked eggs with onion skins achieves a popular tan color? In the North of England these are called pace-eggs or paste-eggs.

Easter Delights Cookbook
A Collection of Easter Recipes
Cookbook Delights Holiday Series-Book 4

Main Dishes

Table of Contents

Page

Did You Know? . . . .

Did you know that Greeks to this day typically dye their Easter eggs red, the color of blood, in recognition of the renewal of life in springtime (and, later, the blood of the sacrificed Christ)? Some also use the color green, in honor of the new foliage emerging after the long "dead" time of winter.

Beef Tenderloin with Roasted Shallots and Bacon

Beef tenderloin makes an elegant main dish. The roasted shallots and bacon combine for a great-tasting sauce.

Ingredients:

¾ lb. shallots, halved lengthwise, peeled
2 Tbs. olive oil
3 c. beef broth
¾ c. port wine
1½ tsp. tomato paste
2 lb. beef tenderloin roast, trimmed
1 tsp. dried thyme
6 slices bacon, cooked, crumbled
4 Tbs. butter, softened, divided
1½ Tbs. all-purpose flour
4 sprigs watercress for garnish
   salt and pepper

Directions:

1. Preheat oven to 375 degrees F.
2. In 9-inch pie pan, toss shallots with oil to coat; season with salt and pepper.
3. Roast in oven until shallots are deep brown and very tender, stirring occasionally, about 30 minutes.
4. In large saucepan combine beef broth and port; bring to a boil, and cook over high heat until volume is reduced by half, about 30 minutes.
5. Whisk in tomato paste and set aside.
6. Pat beef dry; sprinkle with thyme, salt, and pepper.
7. In large roasting pan on stovetop over medium heat, fry bacon until done.
8. Using slotted spoon, transfer bacon to paper towels.
9. Add beef to pan; brown on all sides over medium-high heat, about 7 minutes.

10. Transfer pan to oven, and roast beef until meat thermometer inserted into center registers 125 degrees F. for medium rare, about 25 minutes.
11. Transfer beef to platter; tent loosely with foil.
12. Spoon fat off top of pan drippings in roasting pan.
13. Place pan over high heat on stovetop.
14. Add broth mixture and bring to a boil, stirring to scrape up any browned bits.
15. Transfer to medium saucepan, and bring to a simmer.
16. Mix 1½ tablespoons butter and flour in small bowl to form smooth paste; whisk a bit of broth mixture in, then whisk this mixture into rest of broth mixture, and simmer until sauce thickens.
17. Whisk in remaining butter.
18. Stir in roasted shallots and reserved crumbled bacon.
19. Season with salt and pepper.
20. Cut beef into ½-inch-thick slices.
21. Spoon some sauce over, and garnish with watercress.

Moussaka

This traditional Greek casserole is quite rich and tasty. Serve it with a tossed green salad and a thick, crusty bread to make the meal complete.

Ingredients for tomato sauce:

2   lg. onions
2   Tbs. extra-virgin olive oil
2   Tbs. butter
2   c. mushrooms minced (or substitute 1 lb. lamb)
3   tomatoes, peeled, puréed
3   Tbs. tomato paste

¾ c. dry red wine
½ c. chopped fresh parsley
1 tsp. finely chopped garlic
1 tsp. ground cinnamon
1 Tbs. dried oregano
1 tsp. sugar

Ingredients for white sauce:

4 c. milk
½ c. butter
6 Tbs. all-purpose flour
¼ tsp. white pepper
4 eggs, beaten
2 c. Ricotta cheese

Ingredients for eggplant:

3 lb. eggplant
1½ c. all-purpose flour
1 c. dry bread crumbs
2 c. grated Parmesan cheese
salt
extra-virgin olive oil

Directions for tomato sauce:

1. Peel and mince onions.
2. Sauté in oil and butter over moderate heat until soft and lightly colored, about 8 minutes.
3. Add mushrooms and sauté.
4. Stir in tomatoes, tomato paste, wine, parsley, garlic, cinnamon, oregano, and sugar.
5. Reduce heat to low, and simmer uncovered for 30 to 45 minutes, stirring occasionally, until most of the liquid has evaporated and mixture is quite thick.
6. Remove skillet from heat and let mixture cool completely.

Directions for white sauce:

1. This mixture will overflow all but the largest (professional size) food processors, so use a mixer or blend by hand.
2. Place milk in saucepan, and heat just until tiny bubbles appear along edges; set aside.
3. Melt butter in 3-quart saucepan over very low heat until foamy, being careful not to brown.
4. Slowly add flour, stirring constantly until smooth, 3 to 4 minutes, and still being careful not to let it brown.
5. Add milk slowly, whipping with wire whisk.
6. When mixture is thick and smooth, remove from heat and stir in pepper.
7. Stir Ricotta cheese until smooth and creamy, then gently fold into white sauce.
8. Stir in beaten eggs until thoroughly incorporated.

Directions for eggplant and assembly:

1. Preheat oven to 325 degrees F.
2. Peel eggplant and slice vertically, ⅛ to ¼ inch thick.
3. Sprinkle lightly with salt and let sit for 30 minutes.
4. Rinse eggplant well with cold water; squeeze gently and pat dry.
5. Dredge eggplant in flour, and sauté each slice in olive oil until brown on both sides.
6. Remove and discard any excess oil that has risen to top of tomato mixture.
7. Lightly grease 16 x 10-inch baking pan that is at least 3 inches deep, then sprinkle bottom with a handful of bread crumbs.
8. Place a layer of eggplant in pan, following with a layer of tomato mixture.
9. Sprinkle with bread crumbs and grated Parmesan.
10. Repeat as many times as you have eggplant to last.
11. Pour white sauce over top of all, and bake for 1 hour or until a golden brown crust has formed on top.
12. Remove from oven, and let stand undisturbed 20 to 30 minutes (the delay allows layers to fuse).

Bourbon Pecan Roast Chicken

This flavorful roasted chicken is a special dish to serve on Easter.

Ingredients:

1	whole chicken (about 3 lb.)
½	lemon
4	Tbs. chopped fresh tarragon (or 1½ Tbs. dried)
1	Tbs. chopped fresh rosemary
4	cloves garlic, peeled
3	sm. onions, peeled, cut in half
1	tsp. paprika
½	c. broken pecans
⅔	c. bourbon, divided
	salt and freshly ground pepper

Directions:

1. Preheat oven to 400 degrees F.
2. Wash inside cavity and outside of chicken; pat dry.
3. Rub cavity with cut side of lemon half, and sprinkle cavity with salt and pepper.
4. Fill cavity with tarragon, rosemary, garlic cloves, onions, and paprika.
5. Truss and tie chicken.
6. Gently lift up skin from breast, press pecan bits into meat, and pull skin back into place.
7. Pour ¼ cup bourbon over chicken, and place it on its side in oven.
8. Roast for 20 minutes, turn to other side, add remaining bourbon, baste, and roast another 20 minutes; turn breast side up and roast another 20 minutes or until done.

Fish Florentine

Fish Florentine is elegant and flavorful. It makes a great dish when serving company or just for a special meal.

Ingredients:

1   pkg. frozen spinach (10 oz.), chopped
⅔   c. grated Parmesan cheese, divided
¼   c. plain yogurt
1   egg yolk
1   sm. onion, finely diced
2   tsp. lemon juice
½   tsp. ground nutmeg
4   cod fillets (about 1¼ lb.)
     lemon wedges for garnish

Directions:

1. Cook spinach according to package directions; drain well.
2. Mix together drained spinach, ⅓ cup Parmesan cheese, yogurt, egg yolk, onion, lemon juice, and nutmeg.
3. Line steaming rack with cheesecloth; arrange fish on cheesecloth.
4. Place rack in Dutch oven and cover; steam fish 5 minutes or until fish flakes easily when tested with a fork.
5. Carefully transfer fish to ovenproof serving platter; spoon spinach mixture evenly over each fillet.
6. Sprinkle with remaining ⅓ cup cheese.
7. Broil 3 minutes or until cheese melts.
8. Garnish with lemon wedges and serve.

Rack of Lamb with Tomato
Garlic Rosemary Crust

My son Caleb loves roast lamb, and this is a nice variation. Make sure the lamb is very fresh.

Ingredients:

¼ c. sun-dried tomatoes
1 Tbs. plus 1 tsp. olive oil, divided
1½ lb. rack of lamb, trimmed (8 chops)
2 Tbs. chopped fresh rosemary, divided
¼ c. fresh bread crumbs
2 cloves garlic, peeled, chopped
1 Tbs. Dijon mustard
 salt and pepper to taste

Directions:

1. If using sun-dried tomatoes packed in oil, drain oil before chopping. If using dry tomatoes, place in cup of boiled water until soft, about 5 minutes, then drain and pat dry thoroughly before chopping.
2. Grease roasting pan with 1 teaspoon oil.
3. Place lamb bone side down in pan, and rub with remaining 1 tablespoon oil.
4. Rub 1 tablespoon rosemary all over lamb.
5. Cover and refrigerate at least 30 minutes or overnight.
6. Preheat oven to 400 degrees F.
7. Place remaining rosemary, tomatoes, bread crumbs, garlic, salt, and pepper in food processor; process until well mixed.
8. Using back of spoon, spread mustard along fatty side of lamb, and sprinkle on some black pepper.
9. Press bread crumb-tomato mixture on top of mustard, pressing down firmly.
10. Roast lamb until internal temperature reaches 125 degrees F. for rare, about 30 minutes.

11. Remove pan from oven and let lamb sit, loosely covered with foil, for 5 minutes before carving.
12. Cut vertically between chops to separate; season with salt and pepper.

Yields: 4 servings.

Easter Ham

This makes a moist, delicious Easter ham that will be the highlight of your Easter dinner.

Ingredients:

1   cooked ham half (6 lb.)
1   c. brown sugar, firmly packed
¼   c. real maple syrup
¼   c. Dijon mustard

Directions:

1. Preheat oven to 325 degrees F.
2. Score ham by cutting diagonal lines, ¼-inch deep, into fat to form diamond pattern.
3. Place ham fat side up in shallow roasting pan.
4. Bake 30 minutes.
5. Mix together brown sugar, maple syrup, and mustard in small bowl.
6. Brush ham with half the brown sugar mixture, and return to oven.
7. Bake an additional 30 minutes, then brush with remaining brown sugar mixture.
8. Continue to bake 15 to 20 minutes more or until meat thermometer reads 140 degrees F.
9. Let ham rest for 15 minutes before slicing.

Yields: 12 servings.

Raspberry and Rosemary Grilled Lamb Chops

Raspberry-flavored vinegar and minced rosemary add excellent flavor to these lamb chops.

Ingredients:

- 2 Tbs. raspberry vinegar
- 1 Tbs. Dijon mustard
- 1 Tbs. soy sauce
- 2 Tbs. fresh rosemary, minced (or ½ tsp. dried)
- 1 tsp. olive oil
- 1 clove garlic, minced
- 8 lamb loin chops

Directions:

1. In large, shallow dish whisk together vinegar, mustard, soy sauce, rosemary, oil, and garlic; add lamb chops in single layer, turning to coat well.
2. Cover and marinate in refrigerator at least 2 hours or up to 8 hours, turning occasionally.
3. Discard marinade; place chops on greased grill over medium-high heat, and cook about 5 minutes per side for medium-rare or to desired doneness.
4. Transfer to platter; tent with foil, and let stand 5 minutes before serving.

Did You Know? . . . .

Did you know that one of the oldest ornamentations found on Ukrainian Easter eggs is Beregynia, the goddess of life and fertility, mother of all living things? On Easter eggs she is depicted as a woman with upraised arms.

Roast Leg of Lamb with Herb Crust

This boneless leg of lamb is seasoned just right.

Ingredients:

3	cloves garlic, minced
1	tsp. dried rosemary
1	tsp. dried thyme
½	tsp. black pepper, freshly ground
¼	tsp. salt
2	tsp. lemon juice
3	lb. boneless leg of lamb, trim fat, roll, and tie
½	c. fine, dry, plain bread crumbs
¼	c. minced fresh parsley
⅓	c. water
1	Tbs. olive oil

Directions:

1. In small bowl stir together garlic, rosemary, thyme, pepper, and salt.
2. Rub lemon juice onto lamb, then spread garlic mixture over lamb.
3. Cover and refrigerate for 3 to 4 hours.
4. Preheat oven to 300 degrees F.
5. Coat roasting rack with nonstick spray, and place in roasting pan.
6. Place lamb on rack and roast for 1 hour.
7. In small bowl stir together bread crumbs and parsley; stir in water and oil to make paste.
8. Spread paste on lamb, and bake another 55 to 70 minutes or until meat thermometer registers 145 degrees F. (medium-rare) or 160 degrees F. (medium).

Stewed Lamb

This lamb casserole can be made ahead and is a great-tasting Easter dish.

Ingredients:

- 1   Tbs. butter
- 2   lb. tender lamb, diced
- 2½ c. meat stock
- 1   Tbs. tomato paste
- 12 shallots, peeled
- 1   clove garlic, crushed
- 6   cherry tomatoes
- 2   red bell peppers, seeded, quartered lengthwise
- 1   Tbs. fresh thyme, chopped (or 1 tsp. dried)
    salt and pepper

Directions:

1. Melt butter in saucepan; add lamb and fry over high heat for 2 minutes to seal in juices.
2. Pour meat stock over lamb, stir in tomato paste, and bring to a boil.
3. Add shallots, garlic, tomatoes, and bell peppers; mix well.
4. Add thyme, and season with salt and pepper to taste.
5. Cover and cook over low heat (or in oven preheated to 350 degrees F.) for 1½ hours or until meat is tender and stock is reduced by half.
6. Serve with chunks of warmed bread.

Did You Know?....

Did you know that some believe that a white Christmas will bring a green Easter, and a green Christmas will bring a white Easter?

Roast Pork Tenderloin with Cherry Cranberry Glaze

My daughters Janelle and Marissa love roast pork tenderloin, and this is an attractive and flavorful way to serve it.

Ingredients:

- 2 pork tenderloins
- 1 can unsweetened tart cherries
- 4 tsp. cornstarch
- ¼ c. brown sugar, firmly packed
- ½ c. dried cranberries
- 1 tsp. yellow mustard
  salt and pepper

Directions:

1. Preheat oven to 425 degrees F.
2. Season pork tenderloins with salt and pepper.
3. Roast in shallow roasting pan for 20 to 30 minutes or until internal temperature reads 155 to 160 degrees F.
4. Drain cherries, reserving juice; add enough water to juice to make 1 cup liquid.
5. In small bowl stir cornstarch into 2 tablespoons cherry juice.
6. In small saucepan combine cornstarch mixture with remaining juice, cherries, brown sugar, and cranberries.
7. Cook, stirring, until mixture boils and thickens, then stir in mustard.
8. Pour glaze evenly over tenderloins during last 10 minutes of roasting time.
9. Serve tenderloins sliced.

Garlic Herb Lamb Kabobs

Lamb kabobs are an excellent dish to have on Easter. They are delicious served with wild rice and a green salad. Splurge for dessert, and make it something heavenly!

Ingredients:

2	lb. lamb (boneless leg), cut into 1-in. cubes
1	Tbs. minced garlic
2	tsp. dried oregano
2	tsp. dried rosemary
¼	c. olive oil
¼	c. lemon juice
¾	c. red wine
	assorted vegetables, cut into 1-in. cubes

Directions:

1. Place all ingredients in large, heavy, plastic freezer bag; close tightly and knead until well mixed.
2. Place in refrigerator overnight, turning often.
3. Remove from bag; reserve marinade for basting.
4. Place on skewers, and add vegetables like onion, mushrooms, and bell peppers, if desired.
5. Preheat broiler; place lamb over lowest spot, and slowly cook for 12 to 15 minutes, turning and basting often.

Yields: 6 to 8 servings.

Did You Know? . . . .

Did you know that the Seattle Times has an annual contest of PEEPS® used in photos?

Pies

Table of Contents

Did You Know? . . . .

Did you know that for many, the beautiful trumpet-shaped white flowers of the Easter lily symbolize purity, virtue, innocence, hope, and life—the spiritual essence of Easter?

A Basic Recipe for Pie Crust

This is a very good recipe for a delicious, flaky crust.

Ingredients for single crust:

    1½ c. sifted all-purpose flour
    ½ tsp. salt
    ½ c. shortening
    4-5 Tbs. ice water

Ingredients for double crust:

    2   c. sifted all-purpose flour
    1   tsp. salt
    ⅔ c. shortening
    5-7 Tbs. ice water

Directions for single crust:

1. In large bowl stir together flour and salt.
2. Cut in shortening with pastry blender or mix with fingertips until pieces are size of coarse crumbs.
3. Sprinkle 2 tablespoons ice water over flour mixture, tossing with fork.
4. Add just enough remaining water 1 tablespoon at a time to moisten dough, tossing so dough holds together.
5. Roll pastry into 11-inch circle, and wrap in plastic wrap; refrigerate for 1 hour.
6. Preheat oven to 425 degrees F.
7. Remove plastic wrap from pastry, and fit pastry into a 9-inch pie plate.
8. Fold edge under and then crimp between thumb and forefinger to make fluted crust.
9. For filled pie with an instant or cooked filling (cream-filled, custard-filled, etc.), prick crust all over with fork then bake 15 to 20 minutes until done.
10. If preparing pie with uncooked filling (such as pumpkin), do not prick crust; pour filling into unbaked pastry shell, and then bake as directed.

Directions for double crust:

1. Turn desired filling into pastry-lined pie plate; trim overhanging edge of pastry ½ inch from rim of plate.
2. Cut slits with knife in top crust for steam vents.
3. Place over filling; trim overhanging edge of pastry 1 inch from rim of plate.
4. Fold and roll top edge under lower edge, pressing on rim to seal; flute.
5. Cover fluted edge with 2- to 3-inch-wide strip of aluminum foil to prevent excessive browning.
6. Remove foil during last 15 minutes of baking.

Yields: 1 pie crust (9-inch single or double).

A Basic Cookie or Graham Cracker Crust

This is a great crust for use with cream pies or for an unbaked pie. Use your favorite flavor of cookie to complement your filling, or use graham crackers.

Ingredients:

2   c. cookie or graham cracker crumbs, finely crushed
⅓   c. sugar
½   c. butter, melted

Directions:

1. Combine crumbs, sugar, and butter.
2. Press mixture firmly against bottom and up sides of 9-inch pie plate.
3. Baking is not necessary, but if preferred crust may be baked at 400 degrees F. for 10 minutes.

Yields: 1 pie crust (9-inch).

Banana Cream Pie

My mom and dad used to enjoy banana cream pie, so my mom would make it for family and guests on a frequent basis.

Ingredients:

1   graham cracker crust (recipe page 227)
4   lg. egg yolks
⅔   c. sugar
¼   c. cornstarch
½   tsp. salt
3   c. milk
2   Tbs. butter, softened
1   Tbs. plus 1 tsp. vanilla extract
2   lg. bananas, sliced

Directions:

1. Beat egg yolks with fork in medium bowl; set aside.
2. Mix sugar, cornstarch, and salt in 2-quart saucepan; gradually stir in milk.
3. Cook over medium heat, stirring constantly, until mixture thickens and boils; boil and stir 1 minute.
4. Immediately stir 1 cup of hot mixture gradually into egg yolks, then stir this back into hot mixture in saucepan.
5. Boil and stir 1 minute, then remove from heat.
6. Stir in butter and vanilla.
7. Cool filling to warm temperature.
8. Slice 2 large bananas into prepared pie crust, pour warm filling over bananas, and refrigerate until set.
9. Garnish each serving with a dollop of whipped cream and banana slices if desired.

Yields: 6 to 8 servings.

Chocolate Cheese Pie

This truly decadent cheesecake-type dessert is sure to please all chocoholics everywhere!

Ingredients:

- 1 pkg. cream cheese (8 oz.), softened
- 1 pkg. cream cheese (3 oz.), softened
- ¾ c. sugar
- ½ c. baking cocoa
- 2 eggs
- 1 tsp. vanilla extract
- ½ c. whipping cream, cold
- 1 unbaked chocolate crumb crust (recipe page 227)
- cherry pie filling or sliced fresh fruit

Directions:

1. Preheat oven to 350 degrees F.
2. Beat cream cheese and sugar in large bowl until well blended.
3. Add cocoa; beat until well blended, scraping sides of bowl and beaters frequently.
4. Add eggs and beat well.
5. Stir in vanilla and whipping cream.
6. Pour into prepared crust.
7. Bake 35 to 40 minutes (center will be soft but will set upon cooling).
8. Cool to room temperature.
9. Cover; refrigerate several hours or overnight.
10. When ready to serve, spoon pie filling or fresh fruit over pie.
11. Cover and refrigerate any leftover pie.

Yields: 6 to 8 servings.

Lemon Meringue Pie

My mom also made this pie frequently when I was growing up. I love lemons, and the lemony taste of this pie is always good.

Ingredients for filling:

    3   lg. egg yolks (reserve whites for meringue)
    1½ c. sugar
    ⅓   c. plus 1 Tbsp. cornstarch
    ½   c. water
    3   Tbs. butter
    2   tsp. grated lemon peel
    ½   c. lemon juice
    2   drops yellow food coloring (optional)
    1   baked 9-in. pastry shell (recipe page 226)

Ingredients for meringue:

    3   egg whites, room temperature (reserved from filling)
    1   pinch cream of tartar
    2   Tbs. sugar

Directions for filling:

1. Beat egg yolks with fork in small bowl; set aside.
2. Mix sugar and cornstarch in 2-quart saucepan.
3. Gradually stir in water.
4. Cook over medium heat, stirring constantly, until mixture thickens and boils; boil 1 minute longer.
5. Immediately stir at least half of hot mixture into egg yolks, then stir back into hot mixture in saucepan.
6. Boil and stir 1 minute; remove from heat.
7. Stir in butter, lemon peel, lemon juice, and food coloring if using.
8. Pour hot lemon filling into pie crust.

Directions for meringue:

1. Preheat oven to 350 degrees F.

2. In large bowl beat egg whites and cream of tartar until soft peaks form.
3. Gradually add sugar, and continue beating until stiff peaks form, approximately 1 to 2 minutes.
4. Spread meringue over lemon filling, carefully sealing meringue to edge of crust to prevent shrinking or weeping.
5. Bake 15 minutes or until meringue is light brown.
6. Cool away from draft for 2 hours.
7. Cover and refrigerate cooled pie until serving.
8. Store covered in refrigerator.

Yields: 6 to 8 servings.

Rhubarb Custard Pie

The combination of tart rhubarb and cream custard is delicious.

Ingredients:

4 c. coarsely chopped rhubarb (or unsweetened frozen rhubarb, drained)
1½ c. sugar
4 eggs, lightly beaten
¾ c. half-and-half
⅛ tsp. salt
1½ Tbs. all-purpose flour
1 unbaked 9-in. pastry shell (recipe page 226)

Directions:

1. Preheat oven to 375 degrees F.
2. Combine first 5 ingredients in bowl.
3. Sprinkle flour evenly over pie crust, then add filling.
4. Bake in lower half of oven about 1 hour or until set.

Yields: 6 to 8 servings.

Apple Bourbon Pie

This thick, flavorful pie is a delicious combination of apples, nuts, raisins, and bourbon. For best results soak raisins in bourbon overnight.

Ingredients:

½   c. raisins
½   c. bourbon
3   lb. cooking apples, peeled, cored, sliced
¾   c. sugar
2   Tbs. all-purpose flour
1   tsp. ground cinnamon
⅛   tsp. ground nutmeg
¾   c. toasted pecans or walnuts, chopped
2   tsp. apricot preserves, melted
1   Tbs. buttermilk
1   Tbs. sugar
    pastry for double-crust pie (recipe page 226)

Directions:

1. Preheat oven to 450 degrees F.
2. Combine raisins and bourbon; let soak for at least 2 hours, preferably overnight.
3. Arrange apple slices in steamer basket over boiling water.
4. Cover and steam 10 minutes or until apple slices are just barely tender.
5. Combine flour, cinnamon, and nutmeg in large bowl; add apple slices, raisin mixture, and pecans, stirring to combine.
6. Divide pastry into 2 sections; roll out one half and place in 9-inch pie plate; brush preserves over crust.
7. Spoon apple mixture into crust.
8. Roll out remaining crust, and cut several shapes with 3-inch leaf-shaped cutter.
9. Mark veins on leaves with a pastry cutter or sharp knife.

10. Arrange pastry leaves over apple mixture; brush leaves with buttermilk, and sprinkle sugar over whole top of pie.
11. Cover edges of pie with strips of aluminum foil to prevent excessive browning.
12. Bake on lower rack of oven for 15 minutes.
13. Reduce oven to 350 degrees F., and bake for 30 to 35 minutes more.
14. Remove from oven and serve hot or cool.

Yields: 6 to 8 servings.

Huckleberry Marshmallow Pie

This easy-to-make, great-tasting pie has an attractive presentation. It can be made ahead and kept ready to serve for unexpected company.

Ingredients:

    32 lg. marshmallows
    ½   c. half-and-half
    1   c. whipped cream
    2   c. huckleberries, frozen or fresh
    1   baked pie crust or graham cracker crust shell
        (recipes pages 226 and 227)

Directions:

1. In double boiler melt marshmallows with half-and-half; cool slightly.
2. Blend whipped cream into marshmallow mixture.
3. Gently fold in huckleberries.
4. Pour into baked pastry shell or graham cracker crust, and freeze until ready to serve.

Yields: 6 to 8 servings.

Chocolate Meringue Pie

My family loves chocolate and meringue, so this makes a perfect treat.

Ingredients for pie:

3	egg yolks
1	c. sugar
6	Tbs. all-purpose flour
¼	tsp. salt
3	c. milk, scalded
2	sq. unsweetened chocolate (1 oz. each), chopped
2	Tbs. unsalted butter
½	tsp. vanilla extract
	baked single-crust pastry shell (recipe page 226)

Ingredients for foolproof meringue:

1	Tbs. cornstarch
8	Tbs. sugar, divided
⅓	c. water
4	egg whites
1	pinch salt

Directions for pie:

1. In heatproof bowl lightly beat egg yolks; set aside.
2. In small, heavy saucepan, stir together sugar, flour, and salt.
3. Gradually stir in scalded milk.
4. Cook over medium-low heat, whisking until thickened and bubbly, 6 to 8 minutes.
5. Stir a little of hot mixture into yolks, then stir yolk mixture back into saucepan.
6. Heat over very low heat, stirring for 2 minutes (do not let boil).
7. Remove saucepan from heat.
8. Whisk in chocolate, butter, and vanilla until melted and smooth; scrape into clean bowl.

9. Press piece of plastic wrap directly on surface of filling, and let cool for 10 minutes.
10. Remove plastic wrap, and scrape filling into prepared crust.

Directions for fool proof meringue:

1. Preheat oven to 350 degrees F.
2. In small saucepan stir together cornstarch, 2 tablespoons sugar, and water.
3. Cook over medium heat, stirring occasionally, until mixture comes to a simmer and thickens, 2 to 3 minutes; remove from heat.
4. In large bowl add salt to egg whites; with electric mixer at medium speed, beat just until soft peaks form.
5. Add cornstarch mixture and beat until creamy.
6. Gradually beat in remaining sugar, and continue to beat until soft peaks form, 6 to 8 minutes.
7. Spread meringue over cooled chocolate filling, making sure meringue touches crust edge all the way around.
8. Bake until meringue is golden, 25 to 30 minutes.
9. Cover and refrigerate any leftovers.

Did You Know? . . . .

Did you know that according to a popular piece of folklore, Eostre (Goddess of the Dawn) once saved a bird whose wings had frozen during the winter by turning it into a rabbit? Because the rabbit had once been a bird, it could still lay eggs, and that rabbit became the modern Easter Bunny.

Grasshopper Pie

The trick on this pie is to not rush the process. Chill the cooked marshmallow mixture and the whipped cream. Putting the two mixtures together when they are warm causes the whipped cream to wither, and the pie will not be light and fluffy like it should be.

Ingredients:

- 6 c. miniature marshmallows (about 23 oz.)
- ½ c. cream or milk
- ½ c. green crème de menthe
- 4 Tbs. white crème de cacao
- 2 c. unsweetened whipping cream, divided
- 1 chocolate cookie crust (recipe page 227)
  Sweetened Whipped Cream (recipe page 175)
  chocolate curls

Directions:

1. In large saucepan combine marshmallows and milk.
2. Cook over low heat, stirring constantly, until marshmallows are melted; remove from heat.
3. Cool mixture, stirring every 5 minutes.
4. Combine crème de menthe and crème de cacao; stir into marshmallow mixture and chill.
5. Whip cream until soft peaks form.
6. Fold chilled marshmallow mixture into whipped cream.
7. Turn into prepared crust.
8. Freeze several hours or overnight until firm.
9. Garnish with whipped cream and chocolate curls before serving.

Yields: 6 to 8 servings.

Strawberry Rhubarb Pie

Strawberries and rhubarb combine for a welcome spring treat.

Ingredients:

2½ Tbs. quick-cooking tapioca
1½ Tbs. cornstarch
1   c. sugar
1   c. water
1½ c. strawberries, halved
1½ c. rhubarb cut in 1-in. pieces
1   Tbs. lemon juice
     pastry for double-crust pie (recipe page 226)

Directions:

1. Preheat oven to 425 degrees F.
2. In saucepan cook and stir tapioca, cornstarch, sugar, and water until thick but not boiling; set aside to cool.
3. Stir fruit and lemon juice into cooled mixture.
4. Pour filling into 9-inch pastry-lined pan.
5. Adjust top crust and flute edges; cut 4 to 6 half-inch slits in top for vents.
6. Bake for 50 to 60 minutes or until browned.
7. Remove from oven, and place on wire rack to cool before slicing to serve.

Yields: 6 to 8 servings.

Did You Know? . . . .

Did you know that about 11.5 million Easter lily bulbs were shipped to commercial greenhouses in the United States and Canada in 1996?

Coconut Cream Pie

My mom and dad used to enjoy coconut cream pie, so my mom made it frequently for family and guests.

Ingredients:

    4   lg. egg yolks
    ⅔   c. sugar
    ¼   c. cornstarch
    ½   tsp. salt
    3   c. milk
    2   Tbs. butter, softened
    2   tsp. vanilla extract
    1½   c. flaked coconut, divided
    1   baked 9-in. pastry shell (recipe page 226)
    1   c. Sweetened Whipped Cream (recipe page 175)

Directions:

1. In medium bowl beat egg yolks with fork; set aside.
2. Mix sugar, cornstarch, and salt in 2-quart saucepan.
3. Gradually stir in milk.
4. Cook over medium heat, stirring constantly, until mixture thickens and boils; boil and stir 1 minute.
5. Immediately stir at least half of hot mixture gradually into egg yolks, and then stir back into hot mixture in saucepan.
6. Boil and stir 1 minute; remove from heat.
7. Stir in butter, vanilla, and 1 cup coconut.
8. Pour into prepared crust.
9. Press plastic wrap on filling to prevent a tough layer forming on top.
10. Refrigerate at least 2 hours until set.
11. Remove plastic wrap.
12. Preheat oven to 350 degrees F., and toast remaining ½ cup coconut until lightly browned.
13. Top pie with whipped cream and toasted coconut.
14. Cover and refrigerate pie until serving.

Yields: 6 to 8 servings.

Southern Pecan Pie

This pecan pie is quick to make and will become a favorite with your family.

Ingredients:

1	unbaked 9-in. pastry shell (recipe page 226)
1	c. sugar
2	Tbs. butter, softened
¼	tsp. salt
1	Tbs. all-purpose flour
3	eggs
1	c. white corn syrup
2	tsp. vanilla extract
1	c. chopped pecans

Directions:

1. Preheat oven to 350 degrees F.
2. Cream sugar, butter, salt, and flour together.
3. Add eggs and mix well.
4. Add syrup and vanilla and mix well.
5. Prick pie shell and bake for about 4 minutes.
6. Add chopped pecans to pie shell, then pour in filling.
7. Bake for about 50 minutes.
8. Check after about 15 minutes; if pie crust edges are getting too brown, cover with aluminum foil.

Yields: 6 to 8 servings.

Did You Know?....

Did you know that according to American Greetings, Easter is now the fourth most popular holiday for sending cards, behind Christmas, Valentine's Day, and Mother's Day?

Twin Peaks Cherry Pie

This traditional version of cherry pie is made with cornstarch rather than tapioca.

Ingredients:

2	cans sour cherries (16 oz. each)
1	c. sugar
3	Tbs. cornstarch
⅛	tsp. ground cinnamon
1	pinch salt
1	Tbs. lemon juice
¼	tsp. vanilla extract
	pastry for double-crust pie (recipe page 226)

Directions:

1. Preheat oven to 425 degrees F.
2. Drain cherries, reserving ½ the liquid; pit if needed.
3. Combine sugar, cornstarch, cinnamon, and salt in medium saucepan.
4. Stir in reserved cherry liquid and lemon juice.
5. Bring to boil over medium heat, stirring constantly.
6. Boil 1 minute, remove from heat, and stir in cherries and vanilla; cool completely.
7. Prepare pastry; roll half the pastry on lightly floured surface into 12-inch circle.
8. Line pie plate and leave 1-inch overhang; pour filling into crust.
9. Place other half of rolled out pastry over filling.
10. Fold overhang up over edge and flute; cut slits for steam to escape.
11. Bake for 15 minutes, then reduce oven to 375 degrees F. and bake 30 minutes more, until crust is golden and filling is bubbly.

Yields: 6 to 8 servings.

Easter Delights Cookbook
A Collection of Easter Recipes
Cookbook Delights Holiday Series-Book 4

Preserving

Table of Contents

Page

Did You Know? . . . .

Did you know that Easter is observed by the churches of the West on the first Sunday following the full moon that occurs on or following the spring equinox (March 21)?

A Basic Guide for Canning, Dehydrating, and Freezing

1. Place empty jars in hot, soapy water. Wash well inside and out with brush or soft cloth.
2. Run your finger around rim of each jar, discarding any that are chipped or cracked.
3. Rinse in clean, clear, very hot water, being careful to use tongs to avoid burning skin or fingers.
4. Place upside down on towel or fabric to drain well.
5. Place lids in boiling water bath for 2 minutes to sterilize and keep hot until ready to place on jar rims.
6. Immediately prior to filling jars with hot food, immerse in hot bath for 1 minute to heat jars. Heating jars avoids breakage.
7. If filling with room-temperature food, you need not immerse immediately prior to filling.
8. Fill jars with food to within ½ inch of neck of jars.
9. When ladling liquid over food, fill jars to 1 inch from top rim in each jar. This leaves air allowance for sealing purposes.
10. Wipe rims of jars with damp, clean cloth to remove any particles of food and again check for chips or cracks.
11. Using tongs, place lids from hot bath directly onto jars.
12. Place rings over lids, and using cloth, gloves, or holders, tighten down firmly while hanging onto jars.
13. Do not tighten down too hard as air may become trapped in jars and prevent them from sealing.
14. For fruits, tomatoes, and pickled vegetables, place each jar into water bath canning kettle so water covers jars by at least 1 inch.
15. For vegetables, process them in a pressure canner according to manufacturer's directions.
16. Follow time recommended for food being canned.
17. Do not mix jars of food in same canning kettle as times may vary for each kind of food.
18. At end of time recommended for canning, gently lift each jar out of bath with tongs, and place on protected surface.
19. Turn lids gently to be sure they are firmly tight.

20. Place filled, ringed jars on cloth to cool gradually.
21. Do not disturb rings, lids, or jars until sealed.
22. Lids will show slight indentation when sealed.
23. When cool, wipe jars with damp cloth then label and date each jar.
24. Leave overnight until thoroughly cooled.
25. Jars may then be stored upright on shelves.

Dehydrating

1. Always begin with fresh, good quality food that is clean and inspected for damage.
2. Pretreatment is not necessary, but food that is blanched will keep its color and flavor better. Use the same blanching times as you would for freezing. Fruit, especially, responds to pretreatment.
3. Doing some research on pretreatments may help you decide what procedure you would like to use.
4. You can marinate salt, sweeten, or spice foods before you dehydrate them.
5. Jerky is meat that has been marinated and/or flavored by rubbing spices into it; avoid oil or grease of any kind as it will turn rancid as the food dries.
6. Vegetables and fruit can be treated the same way.
7. Slice or dice food thin and uniform so that it will dehydrate evenly. Uneven thicknesses may cause food to spoil because it did not dry as thoroughly as other parts.
8. Space food on dehydrator tray so that air can move around each piece.
9. Try not to let any piece touch another.
10. Fill your trays with all the same type of food as different foods take different amounts of time to dry.
11. You can, of course, dry different types of food at the same time, but you will have to remember to watch and remove the food that dehydrates more quickly. You can mix different foods in the same dehydrator batch, but do not mix strong vegetables like onions and garlic as other foods will absorb their taste while they are dehydrating.

12. The smaller the pieces, the faster a food will dehydrate. Thin leaves of spinach, celery, etc., will dry fastest. Remove them from the stalks before drying them or they will be overdone, losing flavor and quality. In very warm areas, they might even scorch. If they do, they will taste just like burned food when you rehydrate them.

13. Dense food like carrots will feel very hard when they are ready. Others will be crispy. Usually, a food that is high in fructose (sugar) will be leathery when it is finished dehydrating.

14. Remember that food smells when it is in the process of drying, so outdoors or in the garage is an excellent place to dry a big batch of those onions!

15. Always test each batch to make sure it is "done."

16. You can pasteurize finished food by putting it in a slow oven (150 degrees F.) for a few minutes.

17. Let the food cool before storing.

18. Store in airtight containers to guard against moisture. Jars saved from other food work well as long as they have lids that will keep moisture out.

19. Zip-closure food storage bags work well.

20. Jars of dehydrated carrots, celery, beets, etc., may look cheerful on your countertop, but the colors and flavors will fade. Dehydrated food keeps its color and flavor best if stored in a dark, cool place.

21. Dehydrating food takes time, so do not rush it. When you are all done, you will have a dried food stash to be proud of!

Freezing

1. Wash all containers and lids in hot, soapy water using soft cloth.
2. Rinse well in clear, clean, hot water.
3. Cool and drain well.
4. Place food into container to within 1 inch of rim. This allows for expansion of food during freezing.
5. Wipe rim of container with clean damp cloth, checking for chips or breaks.
6. Be certain cover fits the container snugly to avoid leaks. Burp air from container.
7. If food is hot when placing in container, cool prior to placing in freezer.
8. Label and date each container.
9. Store upright in freezer until frozen solid.

Dehydrated Grapes

These make a great snack for all ages. Select the sweetest grapes you can find for best flavor.

Ingredients:

6   lb. seedless grapes (Sultana, muscatels, or black)

Directions:

1. Seedless grapes are best for drying, but if they are not available, remove seeds before drying.
2. Grapes may be dried in halves or whole. If drying whole, simply parboil for 2 to 3 minutes to 'craze' the skin and make them ready for drying.
3. Place grapes on dehydrator trays (if in halves, cut side down) for 24 to 36 hours.
4. Dry grapes until they look like raisins and are slightly sticky to the touch with no visible moisture.

Dehydrated Onions

Dehydrated onions are great to have on hand to add to your favorite recipes.

Ingredients:

onions, peeled, rinsed

Directions:

1. Slice onions ⅛ to ¼ inch thick, across grain.
2. Onions may be cut into thicker pieces but will be slightly less pungent when dried.
3. Dry at 160 degrees F. for 1 to 2 hours, then at 130 degrees F. until dry.
4. When dried sufficiently, onions should feel like paper.
5. Dried onions will readily reabsorb moisture, causing deterioration during storage; keep packaged in airtight containers in freezer until ready to use.
6. May also be preserved with vacuum sealer and stored on shelf.

Cranberry Pineapple Relish

This is a delicious relish that is a great accompaniment to any meal.

Ingredients:

1   c. cranberries, fresh or frozen
2   c. diced fresh pineapple
1   lg. jalapeño, seeded, diced
1   Tbs. chopped fresh cilantro leaves
2   Tbs. fresh lime juice
2   tsp. light brown sugar
⅛   tsp. salt

Directions:

1. In processor, pulse berries, pineapple, jalapeño, and cilantro to chop to medium consistency.
2. Add lime juice, brown sugar, and salt, blending well.
3. Refrigerate up to 4 hours before eating if using fresh; otherwise, ladle 1 cup of relish into each of 3 freezer containers, burp out air, and freeze for up to 6 months.

Raspberry Fruit Leather

Try homemade raspberry fruit leather for a great snack or lunch treat. You will not want store-bought leather after tasting these.

Ingredients:

2   c. raspberry purée
2   Tbs. honey (optional)

Directions:

1. Mix purée and honey together if using honey.
2. Line cookie sheet or tray with wax paper.
3. Evenly spread purée ¼ inch deep.
4. Place in sun, oven, or dehydrator to dry. (It takes 4 to 10 hours.)
5. Leather is ready when edges are not sticky to the touch.
6. Pull from wax paper while still warm, and roll in plastic wrap.
7. Can be stored for 30 days at room temperature or for months in the refrigerator.

Apple Pie Filling

This makes a great pie filling to have on hand when you need to whip up a homemade pie. It also doubles as a nice homemade gift for holiday gift giving.

Ingredients:

    60 apples (approximate)
    1   c. cornstarch
    1   c. cold water
    4½ c. sugar
    ¼   tsp. ground nutmeg
    1   tsp. salt
    2   tsp. ground cinnamon
    9   c. water
    3   Tbs. lemon juice

Directions:

1. Peel, core, and slice apples.
2. In large pan blend cornstarch in 1 cup cold water.
3. Add sugar, nutmeg, salt, cinnamon, and 9 cups water; cook until thick and bubbly and sugar is dissolved, then stir in lemon juice.
4. Fill quart jars tightly with sliced apples; cover with hot syrup.
5. Process following canning directions on page 242.

Yields: Approximately 12 quarts.

Did You Know? . . . .

Did you know that one of the beliefs about hot cross buns was that eating them on Good Friday served to protect your home from fire?

Dried Apples

These make great portable snacks and are also healthy while still being delicious. Children love them, and they are also great Easter basket fillers in place of candy.

Ingredients:

    3-5 sm. Red Delicious apples, unpeeled, cored
    3   Tbs. lemon juice
    2   c. water
    ¼   tsp. salt

Directions:

1. Preheat oven to 200 degrees F.
2. Slice apples into ⅛-inch-thick pieces.
3. Combine lemon juice and water.
4. Pour over apple slices, stirring so all sides of slices are well coated; drain.
5. Lightly sprinkle salt on both sides of apple slices.
6. Place slices on wire racks that sit on cookie sheets or baking pans to catch drips.
7. Bake for 3½ to 4 hours.
8. Start watching them after about 3 hours; you want them leathery, not crispy.
9. Leaving apples in oven turn off oven and leave overnight or about 8 hours.
10. Store in easy-seal sandwich bags until needed or vacuum pack to keep longer time.

Did You Know? . . . .

Did you know that more than 1 billion Easter eggs are hunted in the United States each year in parks, backyards, and on the White House lawn?

Blueberry Applesauce Fruit Leather

This is excellent fruit leather, and it makes great Easter basket filler. This makes a tart fruit leather, so if you like it sweeter, add more honey.

Ingredients:

- 1   c. blueberry purée
- 1   c. unsweetened applesauce
- 1   Tbs. honey

Directions:

1. In blender or food processor, combine blueberries and applesauce.
2. Process until smooth.
3. Pour mixture through strainer or sieve to remove skin and seeds.
4. Stir in honey.
5. Place mixture in 10-inch skillet.
6. While stirring frequently, cook over very low heat for 1 hour until thickened.
7. Preheat oven to 150 degrees F.
8. Line cookie sheet with parchment paper.
9. Pour thickened mixture onto parchment paper, and spread to form rectangle.
10. Bake 5½ to 6 hours, until fruit sheet is dry enough not to stick to your fingers but moist enough to roll; remove from oven and cool.
11. Placing a potholder in oven door to keep it ajar will help dry the leather by allowing moisture to escape.
12. Once cooked, leather should be rolled in plastic wrap or stored in airtight container to keep.

Dill Pickles

Homemade dill pickles are always a welcome addition on the family table.

Ingredients:

> 4 lb. cucumbers (see note below)
> 2 c. vinegar
> 2 c. water
> 3 Tbs. dill seed (or 9 heads dill weed, fresh or dried)
> 15 whole black peppercorns
> 3 sm. dried red peppers
> 6 tsp. salt

Directions:

1. Note: For whole pickles, small sizes up to 4 inches long are preferred. Larger sizes are usually better sliced, quartered, or halved lengthwise before pickling.
2. Wash cucumbers thoroughly.
3. Combine vinegar and water.
4. Pack cucumbers into clean jars.
5. For each quart, add 1 tablespoon dill seed (or 3 dill heads), 5 whole black peppercorns, 1 red pepper, and 2 teaspoons salt.
6. Fill jars with vinegar-water solution to ½ inch of top.
7. Process for 20 minutes in boiling water bath, following directions for canning found on page 242.

Yields: 3 quarts.

Did You Know? . . . .

Did you know that in past centuries it was considered a lucky omen to meet a lamb, especially at Easter time?

Icicle Sweet Pickles

This method of using ice water makes a great-tasting sweet pickle that is sweet and crisp.

Ingredients:

    1   lg. cucumber
    3   c. white vinegar
    1   c. water
    3   c. sugar
    ¼   c. salt
        ice water

Directions:

1. Peel and remove seeds from cucumber.
2. Cut sticks in ½-inch-wide pieces.
3. Cover with ice water and let stand overnight.
4. Drain and pack in sterilized jars.
5. Boil vinegar, water, sugar, and salt for 3 minutes.
6. Pour over cucumbers to fill jars.
7. Process following canning directions on page 242.
8. Let stand for 6 weeks before using.

Yields: 3 to 4 pints.

Spiced Pickled Beets

If you like the flavor of spicy beets, this recipe is meant for you.

Ingredients:

    4   lb. small beets
    2   c. sugar
    2   c. water
    2   c. vinegar
    1   tsp. ground cloves
    1   tsp. ground allspice
    1   Tbs. ground cinnamon

Directions:

1. Cook beets with roots and about 1 inch of stem until tender, using enough water to cover, about 1 hour.
2. After cooking, place in cool water to hold while slipping skins off.
3. Slice or quarter beets after peeling.
4. Combine sugar, water, vinegar, and spices; add beets and simmer for 15 minutes.
5. Pack beets into hot, sterilized jars, and cover with boiling hot syrup to within ½ inch of rim.
6. Process following canning directions on page 242.

Pickled Chilies

These are great to serve with different meats at your dining table.

Ingredients:

8   oz. whole fresh chilies
3   c. white wine vinegar, divided
1   tsp. salt
4   cloves garlic, peeled
    sprig of bay
    sprig of rosemary

Directions:

1. Select quality chilies; snip off all but base of stems.
2. Bring 1½ cups vinegar and chilies to a boil in pan.
3. Add salt, garlic, bay, and rosemary, and simmer for 6 to 8 minutes.
4. With clean spoon, transfer chilies to sterile jar.
5. Pour in pickling liquid with its herbs, and top up with additional vinegar to cover; allow cooling before sealing.
6. Chilies will be ready within 1 month.

Sweet and Spicy Peach Relish

This tangy relish is great on hot dogs, hamburgers, or cheeseburgers.

Ingredients:

4   lg. semi-ripe peaches, peeled, pitted, finely chopped
1   red bell pepper, finely diced
1   green bell pepper, finely diced
1   red onion, peeled, finely diced
½   c. orange juice
¼   c. virgin olive oil
6   Tbs. fresh lime juice (about 3 limes)
1   Tbs. molasses
1   Tbs. minced red or green chili pepper of your choice
½   c. finely chopped Italian or curly parsley
1   tsp. minced garlic
    salt and freshly cracked black pepper to taste

Directions:

1. In large bowl combine all ingredients and mix well.
2. This relish will keep, covered and refrigerated, about 4 days.

Yields: About 4 cups.

Did You Know? . . . .

Did you know that in large portions of Northern Germany and the eastern part of the Netherlands, Easter Fires are lit on Easter Day at sunset?

Easter Delights Cookbook
A Collection of Easter Recipes
Cookbook Delights Holiday Series-Book 4

Salads

Table of Contents

Page

Did You Know? . . . .

Did you know that the idea of an egg-laying bunny came to the United States in the 18th century? German immigrants in the Pennsylvania Dutch area told their children about the "Osterhase" (Oster–Easter; hase–hare).

Angel Salad with Peach Halo

The combination of different and unusual flavors gives this salad an interesting taste. At the same time it is actually very good.

Ingredients:

1	can sliced cling peaches, drained, syrup reserved
1	Tbs. unflavored gelatin
3	Tbs. lemon juice
2	pkg. cream cheese (3 oz. each), softened
½	c. mayonnaise
¼	tsp. salt
1	tsp. prepared horseradish
½	c. evaporated milk, chilled
½	c. chopped walnuts
¾	c. finely chopped celery
	cherries, peaches, or berries for garnish
	Sweetened Whipped Cream (recipe page 175)

Directions:

1. Heat ¾ cup peach syrup to boiling.
2. Soften gelatin in lemon juice, then dissolve in hot syrup; cool.
3. Mash cream cheese with fork; blend in mayonnaise, salt, and horseradish; blend in gelatin mixture.
4. Whip evaporated milk in chilled bowl until fluffy.
5. Fold in gelatin mixture, walnuts, celery, and peaches.
6. Turn into 8-inch ring mold, and chill until firm.
7. Unmold on greens, decorate with peaches or other fruit, and top with whipped cream.

Baby Greens Candied Pecan Salad

This is a nice salad for your Easter lunch or dinner, with the baby greens and flavors reminiscent of spring.

Ingredients for salad:

6   c. baby greens
2   Tbs. sugar
¼   c. chopped pecans
⅛   c. finely chopped red onion
¼   c. dried cranberries

Ingredients for dressing:

¼   c. olive oil
1½ Tbs. sugar
2   Tbs. balsamic vinegar
¼   tsp. salt
1   pinch black pepper

Directions:

1. Wash salad greens and place in large bowl.
2. Caramelize sugar and pecans in small skillet over medium heat until golden.
3. Pour into small oiled pan and cool.
4. Break apart into bite-size pieces.
5. Whisk dressing ingredients together.
6. Just before serving, toss lettuce with pecans, onions, and cranberries.
7. Toss again with dressing, and place on individual serving plates.

Carrot Salad

This tasty carrot salad will add bright color to your Easter menu.

Ingredients:

1½ lb. carrots, peeled
1   Tbs. olive oil
½   Tbs. red wine vinegar
1   clove garlic, finely chopped
1   pinch black pepper
1   pinch paprika
½   tsp. salt
1   Tbs. chopped fresh parsley
    juice of 1 lemon

Directions:

1. Cut carrots lengthwise into four quartered sections. If they are very long, cut in half to get eight pieces.
2. Place carrots into lightly salted, boiling water, and cook about 5 minutes, until they start to become tender but are still crisp; drain and set aside.
3. Mix olive oil, vinegar, garlic, pepper, paprika, and lemon juice together in saucepan.
4. Return carrot segments to pan, add salt, and gently turn carrots over very low heat for about 5 minutes, until carrots become flavorful.
5. Remove, place into dish, and sprinkle with parsley.
6. Let cool before serving.

Yields: 4 servings.

Make-Ahead Layer Salad

This salad has great color and flavor with the purple grapes, red cabbage, and different cheeses in it. The textures are just as pleasing with everything from smooth to crunchy.

Ingredients:

- 1   pkg. frozen cheese tortellini (9 oz.)
- ½   c. sour cream
- ½   c. buttermilk
- ¼   c. mayonnaise
- ½   c. crumbled Feta cheese
- 1   tsp. sugar
- ¾   tsp. dill weed
- 4   c. baby spinach leaves
- 2   c. chopped red cabbage
- 2   c. cubed Havarti cheese
- 1   c. purple grapes
- 8   slices bacon, cooked crisply, crumbled
- ¾   c. freshly grated Parmesan cheese

Directions:

1. Cook tortellini as directed on package, drain, and cool.
2. Combine sour cream, buttermilk, and mayonnaise; beat well.
3. Stir in Feta cheese, sugar, and dill weed.
4. Combine tortellini with the dressing, mixing well.
5. Place in refrigerator to chill.
6. When ready to serve, layer spinach and cabbage in 13 x 9 x 2-inch glass baking dish.
7. Pour tortellini and dressing over spinach and cabbage.
8. Top with Havarti cheese and grapes.
9. Sprinkle bacon over top, then sprinkle with Parmesan cheese.

Celery Fruit Salad with Raspberry Vinaigrette

Pears, red grapes, and raspberries make a flavorful combination for a great-tasting spring salad.

Ingredients for raspberry vinaigrette:

- ½ c. raspberry vinegar
- ¼ c. raspberries, fresh or frozen
- ¼ c. honey
- ½ c. fresh basil leaves
- ¾ c. extra-virgin olive oil

Ingredients for salad:

- 1⅓ c. raspberry vinaigrette dressing (recipe above)
- 2 Tbs. seedless raspberry jam
- 2 c. celery, cut thin diagonally
- 1 c. fresh pears, unpeeled, cored, sliced
- 1 c. seedless red grapes, cut in halves
- 1 head Boston lettuce
- ½ c. chopped walnuts

Directions for raspberry vinaigrette:

1. In blender or food processor, combine raspberry vinegar, raspberries, honey, and basil; whirl 1 minute or until well blended.
2. With motor on, add olive oil in slow, steady stream, whirling until dressing is smooth.
3. Store, covered, in refrigerator; serve at room temperature.

Directions for salad:

1. In glass measuring cup using wire whisk, combine vinaigrette and jam; set aside.

2. In medium bowl combine celery, pears, and grapes.
3. Add vinaigrette and toss lightly.
4. Line 4 salad plates with lettuce leaves.
5. Spoon celery mixture over lettuce.
6. Sprinkle with chopped walnuts and serve.

Yields: 4 servings' salad; about 1¾ cups dressing.

Baby Lettuce Salad with Tart Raspberry Vinaigrette

This delightful spring salad is a great dish to begin your holiday meal. The raspberry vinegar adds great flavor to this light salad.

Ingredients:

4   Tbs. raspberry vinegar
2   Tbs. olive oil
2   Tbs. rich vegetable stock
1   tsp. chopped fresh oregano
1   tsp. chopped fresh chives
1   dash black pepper
4   c. baby lettuce leaves
    fresh fruit or berries for garnish

Directions:

1. Stir together vinegar, oil, and vegetable stock in small bowl.
2. Add herbs and pepper as close to serving time as possible.
3. Toss dressing with baby lettuce.
4. Place on individual serving plates, and garnish with a slice of fresh fruit or a few berries.

Greek Salad

My daughter Mikayla loves to make this salad and the entire family enjoys eating it. Be sure to use Greek olives for a better flavor.

Ingredients for lemon dressing:

- ¼ c. vegetable oil
- 2 Tbs. lemon juice
- ½ tsp. sugar
- 1½ tsp. Dijon mustard
- ¼ tsp. salt
- ⅛ tsp. pepper

Ingredients for salad:

- 5 c. spinach, torn into bite-size pieces
- 1 head Boston lettuce, torn into bite-size pieces (4 c.)
- ½ c. Feta cheese, crumbled
- 4 green onions, sliced
- 24 pitted Greek olives
- 3 med. tomatoes cut into wedges
- 1 med. cucumber, sliced

Directions:

1. In shaker, combine dressing ingredients; shake together until well blended.
2. Toss dressing and all salad ingredients together.
3. Place on individual serving plates when ready to serve.

Yields: 8 servings.

Marinated Avocado, Jack Cheese, and Tomato Salad

This flavorful salad makes a nice dish for a light lunch or beginning course to a meal. Enjoy this salad with tortilla chips.

Ingredients:

2 lg. avocados, peeled, pitted, diced
8 oz. Jack cheese, diced in large pieces
6 leaves fresh basil, chopped
¼ bunch cilantro, chopped
½ tsp. crushed chilies
2 oz. balsamic vinegar
1 tsp. olive oil
2 tomatoes, sliced
  salt and pepper
  tortilla chips

Directions:

1. Combine avocado, cheese, basil, cilantro, crushed chilies, vinegar, and olive oil, blending well.
2. Arrange tomatoes on plate in overlapping circle.
3. Place avocado-cheese mixture over top of tomatoes.
4. Garnish with tortilla chips around edges.

Did You Know? . . . .

Did you know that Eastertide, the season of Easter, begins on Easter Sunday and lasts until the day of Pentecost, seven weeks later?

Spaghetti Squash and Avocado Salad

If you want a unique salad with lots of color, try this recipe. Make sure you prepare the vinaigrette 24 hours ahead of time in order for the flavors to meld.

Ingredients for avocado oil vinaigrette:

¾ c. avocado oil (or vegetable oil)
¼ c. white wine vinegar
3   cloves garlic, crushed
1   tsp. dried oregano
1   tsp. dried sweet basil
1   tsp. dried rosemary
1   tsp. dry mustard
1   tsp. Worcestershire sauce
    salt and pepper

Ingredients for salad:

1   med. spaghetti squash
6   mushrooms, sliced
½ red bell pepper, diced
½ yellow bell pepper, diced
1   can sliced black olives
2   avocados, peeled, pitted, diced

Directions for avocado oil vinaigrette:

1. Place oil, vinegar, garlic, oregano, sweet basil, rosemary, mustard, and Worcestershire sauce in shaker; salt and pepper to taste.
2. Place lid on shaker and blend well.
3. Refrigerate at least 24 hours before using.

Directions for salad:

1. Halve squash lengthwise and scoop out seeds.
2. Place halves cut side down in large saucepan; add water to depth of 2 inches.

3. Cover and bring to a boil; reduce heat and simmer squash 20 minutes.
4. Drain water, cool squash, and gently pull strands from skins.
5. Place in large bowl and lightly toss squash, mushrooms, peppers, olives, and avocados to blend ingredients.
6. Place on individual serving plates and pour vinaigrette over salad to serve.

Mango Avocado Salad

This mango avocado salad is really refreshing served with Papaya Seed Dressing. It is great for Easter dinner.

Ingredients:

1   mango, chopped
1   red pepper, diced
1   tomato, diced
2   avocados, chopped
¼   c. diced red onions
1   dash garlic salt
     Papaya Seed Dressing (recipe page 192)

Directions:

1. Combine mango, red pepper, tomato, avocados, and onions in medium bowl, or arrange on individual plates.
2. Sprinkle with dash of garlic salt.
3. Cover and chill 20 to 30 minutes.
4. When ready to serve, remove from refrigerator and top with Papaya Seed Dressing or your favorite fruit-flavored vinaigrette.

Spiced Cherry Salad

This is a refreshing spring salad to serve at Easter. Enjoy the colors, textures, and flavors.

Ingredients:

1	c. dried tart cherries
1	can mandarin orange sections (11 oz.), drained
2	kiwifruits, peeled, sliced
¼	c. orange juice
¼	c. powdered sugar, sifted
¼	tsp. ground cinnamon
¼	c. slivered almonds, toasted

Directions:

1. Place dried cherries, mandarin orange sections, and kiwi slices in salad bowl.
2. Combine orange juice, powdered sugar, and cinnamon in small bowl; mix thoroughly.
3. Pour orange juice mixture over fruit mixture; toss gently to combine flavors.
4. Cover and refrigerate 1 to 2 hours, stirring occasionally.
5. When ready to serve, remove from refrigerator and sprinkle with toasted almonds.

Did You Know? . . . .

Did you know that Belgium shares the same Easter traditions as North America, but sometimes it is said that the Bells of Rome bring the Easter eggs together with the Easter Bunny?

Easter Delights Cookbook
A Collection of Easter Recipes
Cookbook Delights Holiday Series-Book 4

Side Dishes

Table of Contents

Page

Did You Know? . . . .

Did you know that beeping Easter eggs are Easter eggs that emit various clicks and noises so that visually-impaired children can hunt for Easter eggs? Some make a single, high-pitched sound and others play a melody.

Baked Acorn Squash

This delicious, easy side dish is great anytime of the year. My daughter Marissa especially enjoys this side dish.

Ingredients:

1	acorn squash
2	pats butter
2	tsp. honey or maple syrup
2	Tbs. brown sugar
	salt and pepper

Directions:

1. Preheat oven to 375 degrees F.
2. Cut squash in half and scoop seeds out with spoon.
3. Slice very small amount off bottom of each half without cutting a hole into squash to assist squash in sitting upright while baking.
4. Add 1 pat butter, 1 teaspoon honey or maple syrup, 1 tablespoon brown sugar, salt, and pepper to hollow scoop of each half.
5. Place upright on greased cookie sheet, and roast for 50 to 60 minutes or until flesh is tender when poked with fork.
6. Remove from oven and place upright on serving platter to serve.

Did You Know?....

Did you know that today Easter is commercially important, seeing wide sales of greeting cards and confectionery such as chocolate Easter eggs, marshmallow bunnies, PEEPS®, and jelly beans?

Candied Yams

These are delicious and perfect for vegetarians.   We add marshmallows on some for the younger children.

Ingredients:

6   lg. yams
½   c. butter
1   c. brown sugar, firmly packed
¼   c. water
2   Tbs. vanilla extract
    miniature marshmallows (optional)

Directions:

1. Preheat oven to 350 degrees F.
2. Boil yams in skins until about half done.
3. Drain water from yams, remove skins, and cut in lengthwise slices.
4. Place slices in greased baking dish, and dot with butter.
5. Make syrup by boiling together brown sugar, water, and vanilla; pour over yam slices.
6. Bake 45 to 50 minutes, until tender, basting frequently with syrup.
7. If desired place miniature marshmallows over top, and return to oven under broiler to melt and brown marshmallows.

Did You Know?....

Did you know that another food associated with Easter is the pretzel? Its twisted shape symbolizes arms crossed in prayer.

Chestnut Stuffing

Chestnuts are delicious alone and are also great in stuffing and dressings. This excellent chestnut stuffing goes well with turkey, chicken, or your favorite meat.

Ingredients:

- 2   qt. chestnuts (about 4 lb.)
- 4   tsp. olive oil or salad oil
- 6   c. beef broth
- 1   onion, chopped
- 2   Tbs. butter
- ½   lb. sausage
- 1   tsp. chopped chives
- ½   tsp. powdered thyme
- ¼   tsp. powdered marjoram
- 1   tsp. chopped parsley
- ¾   c. soft bread crumbs
-      salt and pepper to taste

Directions:

1. Cut gashes in flat side of each chestnut.
2. In large skillet heat oil; add chestnuts, and cook over brisk heat for 3 minutes, stirring or shaking pan constantly.
3. Drain and let cool; remove shells and inner skins.
4. Add beef broth, and cook chestnuts about 20 minutes or until tender.
5. Drain, reserving broth for soup.
6. Chop half the nuts coarsely and mash the rest; set aside.
7. Preheat oven to 350 degrees F.
8. In skillet, cook onion in butter until golden brown.
9. Add sausage, chives, thyme, marjoram, parsley, and salt and pepper to taste; cook, stirring constantly, 4 to 5 minutes.

10. Soften bread crumbs in milk or water; press out excess liquid; add to sausage mixture along with chestnuts.
11. Transfer to oiled casserole dish; cover and bake 20 minutes; uncover and bake 15 minutes more.

Honeyed Carrots

Baby carrots make an excellent side dish for your Easter meal.

Ingredients:

4   Tbs. olive oil
2   lb. fresh baby carrots
4   Tbs. honey
2   Tbs. butter, melted
    salt and freshly ground black pepper

Directions:

1. Heat large, heavy skillet over low heat.
2. Add oil and carrots; season liberally with salt and pepper.
3. Cook for 15 to 20 minutes, turning occasionally, until carrots are nicely browned.
4. Mix honey and butter together, and drizzle over carrots, cooking until sauce is melted and smooth.

Yields: 8 servings.

Did You Know?....

Did you know that in Hungary on Easter Monday (where it is called Ducking Monday), perfume or perfumed water is often sprinkled in exchange for an Easter egg?

Cornbread Stuffing

Our family likes this cornbread stuffing. It is a tasty change from the usual bread stuffing.

Ingredients:

½   c. butter
2   c. chopped onion
1   c. chopped celery
2   c. chicken broth (or vegetable broth for vegetarians)
1   can whole kernel corn
2   cans diced green chilies (4 oz. each)
3   Tbs. chopped fresh parsley
½   tsp. paprika
½   tsp. salt
⅛   tsp. black pepper
¼   tsp. dried oregano
6   c. crumbled cornbread (recipe page 97)
1   c. chopped pecans

Directions:

1. Preheat oven to 350 degrees F.
2. In large skillet, melt butter over low heat.
3. Sauté onion and celery in butter until tender, 5 to 8 minutes.
4. Stir in broth, corn, green chilies, parsley, paprika, salt, pepper, and oregano.
5. Add cornbread and pecans; mix to incorporate.
6. Spoon into 2½-quart buttered baking dish, and bake 45 to 60 minutes or until golden brown.

Fried Rice

My children love fried rice. We serve it at Easter, and they add their favorite topping–soy sauce or turkey gravy.

Ingredients:

1	c. medium-grain rice
2	Tbs. oil
1	carrot, finely chopped
3	cabbage leaves, finely chopped
6	fresh green beans, finely chopped
1	bunch spring onions, finely chopped
½	tsp. salt
1	tsp. soy sauce
2	eggs, beaten, scrambled, chopped

Directions:

1. Boil rice to almost done; drain and cool on plate.
2. Heat oil in wok or skillet; add carrot, cabbage, and beans; stir-fry until crisp.
3. Add spring onions, salt, and soy sauce.
4. Mix well then add rice; stir in eggs, and gently stir- fry to coat and blend ingredients; serve while hot.

Did You Know? . . . .

Did you know that a tradition exists in some parts of the United Kingdom (such as Scotland and Northeast England) of rolling painted eggs down steep hills on Easter Sunday?

Giblet Stuffing

This makes a savory, multifaceted stuffing that will impress your guests.

Ingredients:

1	Tbs. vegetable oil
1	carrot, chopped
2	onions, chopped, divided
1	can chicken broth (13¾ oz.)
¼	tsp. dried thyme
¼	tsp. salt
8	peppercorns
8	Tbs. unsalted butter
3	stalks celery, chopped
15	oz. seasoned stuffing cubes
¼	c. chopped fresh parsley
3	c. turkey stock
2	tsp. poultry seasoning
	turkey giblets and neck
	water
	salt and pepper to taste

Directions:

1. Remove giblets from cavity of turkey.
2. Chop turkey neck into 2-inch pieces.
3. Trim liver and put in refrigerator.
4. Heat vegetable oil in large saucepan over medium-high heat; add turkey neck pieces and gizzard.
5. Sauté for about 10 minutes or until browned on all sides.
6. Add carrot, 1 onion, chicken broth, and enough cold water to cover giblet mixture by 1 inch; bring to a simmer.
7. Skim off foam that rises to surface during cooking.
8. Add thyme, salt, and peppercorns.
9. Reduce heat to low, and simmer with saucepan partially covered, about 2 hours.

1. Add turkey liver, and simmer an additional 15 to 20 minutes.
2. Strain mixture and cool giblets.
3. Pull meat off turkey neck.
4. Chop neck meat, gizzard, and liver; set aside.
5. In large skillet, melt butter over medium heat.
6. Add celery and remaining onion; cook 10 minutes, stirring occasionally.
7. Preheat oven to 350 degrees F.
8. Place vegetables and butter in mixing bowl, and add bread and parsley.
9. Drizzle stock over bread mixture until it is just moist.
10. Season with poultry seasoning, and salt and pepper to taste.
11. Gently toss in neck meat, gizzard, and liver.
12. Place in casserole dish, pour an extra ½ cup of stock over top, and bake, covered, for 45 minutes or until hot.

Simple Baby Asparagus

These are easy, delicious, and make a healthy and colorful side dish.

Ingredients:

    3   Tbs. butter
    2   lb. baby asparagus, trimmed
        salt and pepper

Directions:

1. Melt butter in large, heavy skillet over low heat.
2. Add asparagus, and cook until tender but still very crisp and bright green, 4 to 5 minutes
3. Season to taste with salt and pepper.
4. Serve while hot.

Yields: 8 servings.

Parmesan Polenta

Polenta makes a unique and excellent side dish. Try it and enjoy.

Ingredients:

> 4   c. water
> 1   c. yellow cornmeal
> 4   Tbs. butter
> ¾   c. grated fresh Parmesan cheese, divided
>   salt and pepper to taste

Directions:

1. Combine water, cornmeal, and salt in large, heavy saucepan.
2. Whisking constantly, bring to a boil over medium-high heat.
3. Reduce heat to low and simmer, stirring occasionally, for 15 to 20 minutes or until very thick.
4. Whisk in butter, 6 tablespoons Parmesan, and pepper to taste.
5. Spoon into ovenproof serving dish.
6. Sprinkle remaining cheese on top of polenta.
7. Cool to room temperature and tightly wrap with heavy-duty aluminum foil.
8. Freeze for up to 3 months.
9. To reheat, bake at 350 degrees F. for 30 minutes or until piping hot before serving.

Yields: 8 servings.

Potatoes Au Gratin

This is a version of scalloped potatoes with cheddar cheese melted in. Most of our family prefers au gratin potatoes, so we rotate them in frequently.

Ingredients:

   2   lb. potatoes, peeled
   2   Tbs. butter
  ¼ c. all-purpose flour
   2   c. milk, heated
  ⅓ tsp. salt
  ¼ tsp. pepper
  ½ lb. cheddar cheese, shredded
  ¾ c. dry bread crumbs
   2   Tbs. butter, melted

Directions:

1. Preheat oven to 375 degrees F.
2. Cook potatoes in boiling salted water until tender; drain and dice.
3. Meanwhile, melt butter then stir in flour.
4. Add milk; cook and stir until smooth and thick, about 20 minutes.
5. Add seasonings, then stir in cheese; blend.
6. Pour sauce over potatoes; stir to blend.
7. Spoon mixture into 13 x 9 x 2-inch casserole.
8. Combine crumbs and melted butter, stirring until blended.
9. Sprinkle over potatoes.
10. Bake for 25 minutes or until bubbly hot.
11. Remove from oven and serve while hot.

Scalloped Potatoes

This is another easy-to-make scalloped potato recipe. These are a great accompaniment to ham.

Ingredients:

> 1½ lb. red potatoes
> 1   c. butter, divided
> ½   c. all-purpose flour
> ½   tsp. salt
> ½   tsp. pepper
> ½   c. milk, scalded
> 1½ c. toasted or dried bread crumbs

Directions:

1. Preheat oven to 350 degrees F.
2. Peel and slice potatoes, or leave peels on and just slice.
3. Arrange in buttered 13 x 9 x 2-inch baking pan.
4. Melt ½ cup butter over medium heat, and then stir in flour and seasonings.
5. To melted butter mixture, gradually add milk, cooking until thickened, stirring constantly.
6. Pour thickened white sauce over potatoes, and bake for 1 hour.
7. Cover with bread crumbs, drizzle bread crumbs with remaining ½ cup melted butter, and bake about 1 hour longer or until potatoes are tender.

Yields: 4 servings.

Did You Know? . . . .

Did you know that the ingredients in PEEPS® are marshmallow, sugar, gelatin, and carnauba wax?

Sweet and Nutty Holiday Peas

These peas make a colorful side dish for your Easter menu.

Ingredients:

2	lb. sugar snap peas
3	Tbs. butter
2	Tbs. honey
2	tsp. Dijon mustard
¾	c. salted peanuts, coarsely chopped

Directions:

1. Steam or blanch peas in salted water for a few minutes to cook them slightly, and then plunge into ice water to retain bright green color. (Do not overcook; they should be bright green but still very crisp.)
2. In small saucepan or microwave-safe bowl, melt butter, and then mix in honey and mustard until smooth.
3. Pour over peas, add peanuts, and toss; transfer to serving dish and serve while hot.

Yields: 6 servings.

Did You Know? . . . .

Did you know that in Ukraine and other Slavic countries, a batik-like decorating process known as "pysanka" produces intricate, brilliantly-colored eggs?

Garlic Bacon Cheddar Mashed Potatoes

These delicious potatoes make a very hearty side dish. They are just as delicious without bacon, for any vegetarians in your household.

Ingredients:

- 3 lb. russet potatoes, peeled, cut into 1-in. cubes
- 5 cloves garlic, quartered
- 10 slices bacon (leave out for vegetarian)
- 1 c. buttermilk, warm
- ¼ c. chopped fresh chives
- 1¼ c. shredded cheddar cheese
- salt and pepper

Directions:

1. Place potatoes and garlic in large, heavy saucepan, and add enough cold water to cover.
2. Bring to a boil over high heat.
3. Reduce heat to medium-high, cover, and cook for 15 to 20 minutes or until potatoes are fork tender; drain well.
4. Cook bacon, crumble, and set aside.
5. Return potatoes to saucepan and toss to evaporate any water.
6. Coarsely mash potatoes with buttermilk, making sure to leave majority of potatoes in large chunks.
7. Add chives and bacon; salt and pepper to taste.
8. Sprinkle shredded cheddar cheese over top, and lightly toss with potato mixture.
9. Serve while hot.

Yields: 12 servings.

Easter Delights Cookbook
A Collection of Easter Recipes
Cookbook Delights Holiday Series-Book 4

Soups

Table of Contents

Page

Did You Know? . . . .

Did you know that according to the U.S. Department of Agriculture, Easter lilies had a wholesale value of $37.4 million in 1995?

African Peanut Soup

This is a thick, hearty soup. Serve it topped with plenty of chopped scallions and chopped peanuts.

Ingredients:

2	c. chopped onion
1	Tbs. vegetable oil
½	tsp. cayenne pepper
1	tsp. fresh ginger, peeled, grated
1	c. chopped carrots
2	c. chopped sweet potatoes
4	c. vegetable stock or water
2	c. tomato juice
1	c. smooth peanut butter
1	Tbs. sugar
¼	c. chopped scallions
½	. roasted peanuts

Directions:

1. Sauté onion in oil until translucent.
2. Add cayenne, ginger, and carrots; sauté lightly.
3. Mix in sweet potatoes and stock; bring to a boil, and simmer 15 minutes until vegetables are tender.
4. Purée vegetables in blender with tomato juice and some cooking liquid if necessary; return purée to pot.
5. Stir in peanut butter until smooth; check sweetness and add sugar if necessary.
6. Add scallions and roasted peanuts.
7. Reheat gently; add more water, stock, or tomato juice to make thinner soup if desired.

Did You Know? . . . .

Did you know that Red PEEPS® chicks are found only at Target stores?

Avgolemon Soup

This is one of my very favorite soups. I love the combination of chicken broth and lemon. It is also great without the lemon. Children enjoy its refreshing taste!

Ingredients:

    12 c. homemade chicken broth or canned
    1⅛ c. long-grain white rice
    24 egg yolks
    1   c. fresh lemon juice
         kosher salt
         freshly ground black pepper

Directions:

1. In medium saucepan bring stock to a boil.
2. Stir in rice; cover and cook until tender, about 15 to 20 minutes.
3. Meanwhile, beat egg yolks and lemon juice together in large bowl.
4. When rice is tender, slowly ladle half the hot broth into yolks to temper them, whisking constantly.
5. Whisk egg yolk mixture back into broth, and place over low heat.
6. Cook, stirring constantly, just long enough to thicken soup; do not boil.
7. Remove from heat, and season to taste with salt and pepper.
8. Ladle into bowls and serve while hot.

Did You Know? . . . .

Did you know that an American belief is that good luck can be ensured for the year by wearing three new things on Easter Sunday?

Cream of Artichoke Soup

This soup tastes like both cream of chicken and artichoke soup at the same time. Garnish with Parmesan-flavored croutons.

Ingredients:

4	whole artichokes
2	c. water
2	c. chicken stock
½	c. dry vermouth
1	potato, diced
1	sm. carrot, diced
1	onion, chopped
1	sm. stalk celery, diced
2	cloves garlic, minced
2	bay leaves
½	tsp. dried marjoram
1	c. heavy whipping cream
¼	c. grated Romano cheese
	salt to taste
	freshly ground black pepper to taste

Directions:

1. Steam artichokes in 2 cups water until tender, about 45 minutes; drain, reserving liquid.
2. Allow artichokes to cool.
3. Scrape flesh from bottom third of each leaf, and place in medium soup pot along with artichoke liquid.
4. Remove fuzzy choke from each artichoke bottom and discard.
5. Coarsely dice artichoke bottoms, and place in soup pot.
6. Add chicken stock, vermouth, potato, carrot, onion, celery, garlic, bay leaves, and marjoram.
7. Simmer until vegetables are very tender and liquid is reduced by ⅓, about 45 minutes.
8. Purée soup in blender and return to pot.
9. Add cream and cheese; heat through but do not allow to boil.
10. Add salt and pepper to taste.

Yields: 4 servings.

Mom's Vegetarian-Style Corn Chowder

This is a thick, creamy soup that my children always ask me to make for them. All of them love it, and we think you will too!

Ingredients:

- ¼ c. chopped onion
- 3 Tbs. butter
- 2 c. sliced celery
- 2 c. sliced carrots
- 2 c. diced red potatoes
- 2 c. half-and-half
- 2 c. whipping cream
- 2 c. frozen corn
- 1 tsp. salt
- ⅛ tsp. pepper
- ¼ tsp. garlic salt

Directions:

1. Fry onion in butter until golden brown; add celery and carrots and sauté until tender.
2. In saucepan cook potatoes until soft, then drain, reserving 2 cups potato water.
3. Mix potato water with half-and-half and cream; add potatoes, sautéed vegetables, corn, and seasonings.
4. Bring to a boil, and then serve in bowls while hot.

Cream of Mushroom Soup

This rich, heavy soup can be a meal in itself. When possible, I try to use a variety of mushrooms for a varied, interesting flavor.

Ingredients:

3	lb. mushrooms, any variety
1½	c. butter
3	tsp. fresh lemon juice
3	sm. onions, diced
1	c. all-purpose flour
10½	c. vegetable broth
3	tsp. salt
¾	tsp. pepper
3	c. heavy cream
	chives or chopped green onions

Directions:

1. Remove stem end of mushrooms; set aside.
2. Slice mushroom caps thinly, crosswise.
3. In large Dutch oven or large soup pot, melt butter over medium-high heat.
4. Add sliced mushroom caps and lemon juice; sauté until mushrooms are tender.
5. Reduce heat to low.
6. With slotted spoon, transfer mushrooms to small plate.
7. Add onions and mushroom stems to Dutch oven; cook until onions are tender.
8. Stir in flour until blended; cook 1 minute, stirring constantly.
9. Gradually stir in broth, stirring constantly until thickened, and then cool to lukewarm.
10. Purée mixture with an immersion blender, or transfer to regular blender in batches until all is puréed.
11. Add salt, pepper, cream, and sautéed mushrooms.
12. Reheat until warm, then serve, garnished with chives or green onion.

Thai Chicken Soup

This is a favorite recipe for our family. You can delete the chicken and the fish sauce for a vegetarian soup.

Ingredients:

2   cans coconut milk
1   Tbs. red curry paste, less for milder soup
4   chicken breasts, sliced in strips
2   cans straw mushrooms
¼   c. fish sauce
    small amount of lime juice or 2 lime leaves
    cashews
    cilantro

Directions:

1. Mix coconut milk, red curry paste, and chicken together in saucepan.
2. Cook about 15 minutes.
3. Add straw mushrooms, then add fish sauce after 1 minute.
4. Add lime juice at the end.
5. Ladle into bowls, and sprinkle with cashews and cilantro.
6. Serve immediately while hot.

French Onion Soup

This is a delightful soup as a first course, light yet satisfying. If the flavor of the soup is not strong enough, just add more bouillon cubes to desired taste.

Ingredients:

1-2 lg. red onions, sliced
3 lg. cloves garlic, minced
½ c. red wine
1   tsp. black pepper
6   c. water
6   beef bouillon cubes
3   c. croutons
6   pieces mozzarella cheese, thinly sliced
     fresh parsley, chopped

Directions:

1. In large saucepan combine onions, garlic, red wine, and pepper.
2. Cover, and cook at medium until onions become transparent, stirring occasionally.
3. Add water and bouillon cubes; reduce heat to medium-low and simmer 20 to 25 minutes.
4. Pour soup into bowl until it is ⅛ inch from the top; place croutons on top and a slice of cheese over top of croutons.
5. Place bowl under broiler and cook 2 to 3 minutes, until cheese is melted.
6. Use caution as bowl will be very hot!
7. To serve, sprinkle fresh parsley on top.

Yields: 6 servings.

Greek Lemon Chicken Soup

This is a hearty version of the classic Greek soup.

Ingredients:

8	c. chicken broth
½	c. lemon juice
¼	tsp. pepper
½	c. uncooked rice
1	med. carrot, shredded
4	egg yolks, beaten
1	c. cooked chicken, chopped
1	lemon, thinly sliced

Directions:

1. Bring broth, lemon juice, and pepper to a boil in large saucepan.
2. Add rice and carrot; reduce heat and simmer 25 minutes.
3. Stir small amount of soup into beaten egg yolks.
4. Stir egg mixture back into soup, and add chicken.
5. Cook until heated through, stirring frequently; do not boil.
6. Ladle into soup bowls and garnish each with a lemon slice.

Yields: 8 servings.

Did You Know? . . . .

Did you know that Austrian artists design patterns by fastening ferns and tiny plants around eggs, which are then boiled? The plants are then removed revealing a striking white pattern.

Lobster Bisque

This wonderful, creamy, thick soup that is full of flavor is a complement to any meal.

Ingredients:

2 cans lobster meat (6 oz. each)
½ c. chopped onion
¾ c. butter
¾ c. all-purpose flour, sifted
2 cans condensed chicken broth (10½ oz. each)
¾ c. dry sherry
3 c. light cream
2 Tbs. tomato paste
½ tsp. salt
1 dash pepper

Directions:

1. Drain lobster, removing any cartilage.
2. Set aside several large pieces for garnish, then dice remainder.
3. In large saucepan sauté onion in butter until soft.
4. Stir in flour; cook, stirring constantly, until bubbly.
5. Stir in chicken broth.
6. Continue cooking and stirring until mixture thickens and boils, about 1 minute.
7. Stir in diced lobster and sherry; cover and simmer 20 minutes.
8. Blend in cream, tomato paste, salt, and pepper; heat slowly just until hot.
9. Ladle into tureen; float saved pieces of lobster on top.

Yields: 8 servings.

Mom's Yugoslavian Soup

This is a good recipe to have on hand on Good Friday because of fasting choices. It is a simple soup made by poor people who have little food, but it is surprisingly good.

Ingredients:

    2   c. all-purpose flour
    8   eggs
    1   tsp. salt
    ¼   tsp. pepper
    2   qt. boiling water
    ¼   c. butter
         salt and pepper to taste

Directions:

1. Combine flour, eggs, 1 teaspoon salt, and ¼ teaspoon pepper to make dough.
2. Make dough with hands, using more flour and eggs as needed.
3. Bring 2 quarts of water to a boil.
4. Meanwhile, roll and cut dough into small pieces.
5. Melt butter in deep skillet; add dough pieces and brown until almost black.
6. When nearly black, add boiling water and cook about 10 minutes; add salt and pepper to taste.
7. Ladle into bowls and serve while hot.

Did You Know? . . . .

Did you know that the Easter lily has the narrowest holiday sales window, typically only 2 weeks?

Chicken Noodle Soup

Homemade chicken soup enhanced with homemade noodles is always a welcome treat.

Ingredients:

1	c. chopped celery
1	c. chopped onion
¼	c. butter
12	c. water
1	c. diced carrots
3	Tbs. chicken bouillon
½	tsp. marjoram leaves
¼	tsp. pepper
1	bay leaf
6	oz. egg noodles (homemade if possible)
4	c. cooked chicken, diced
¼	c. chopped fresh parsley, divided

Directions:

1. In large Dutch oven sauté celery and onion in butter until tender.
2. Add water, carrots, bouillon, marjoram, pepper, and bay leaf; bring to a boil then reduce heat.
3. Simmer covered for 30 minutes.
4. Remove bay leaf; add noodles, chicken, and half the parsley.
5. Cook 10 minutes longer or until noodles are tender, stirring occasionally.
6. Remove from heat, ladle into bowls, and sprinkle with remaining parsley; serve while hot.

Easter Delights Cookbook
A Collection of Easter Recipes
Cookbook Delights Holiday Series-Book 4

Wines and Spirits

Table of Contents

Page

About Cooking with Alcohol

Some recipes in this cookbook contain, among other ingredients, liquors. It is for the purpose of obtaining desired flavor and achieving culinary appreciation and not to be abused in any way. In cooking and baking, alcohol evaporates and only the flavor may be enjoyed. When mixed in cold, however, such as in desserts, caution must be exercised. These recipes are intended for people who may consume small amounts of alcohol in a responsible and safe manner.

I live in Washington State, and we are proud of our wine production. Washington State is rapidly gaining prestige as a premier wine producer. Do enjoy the art of wine tasting, and enjoy the completeness and uniqueness of each wine. It is an art to enjoy and savor in moderation.

If consumption of even small amounts of alcoholic ingredients presents a problem, in whatever form, please substitute coffee flavor syrups, found in coffee sections of supermarkets. For example, instead of Southern Comfort liqueur, substitute with Irish Cream or Amaretto Syrup.

Karen Jean Matsko Hood

Black Russian

This drink is easy and refreshing. Enjoy!

Ingredients:

¾ oz. coffee liqueur
1½ oz. vodka
    ice cubes

Directions:

1. Pour ingredients over ice cubes in old-fashioned glass and serve.

Pink Squirrel

This drink has a spring pink color and is a refreshing after-dinner Easter drink.

Ingredients:

    1   oz. crème de noyaux
    1   oz. white crème de cacao
    1   oz. cream
        ice

Directions:

1. Mix ingredients with ice in shaker or blender.
2. Strain into chilled cocktail glass.

Easter Bonnets

This is a special spring drink for Easter dinner.

Ingredients:

    1½ oz. vodka
    1½ oz. apricot brandy
    1½ oz. peach brandy
    ¼ lemon, juiced
    1   orange slice
        ice
        champagne

Directions:

1. Place first 4 ingredients in tall glass.
2. Add ice to top of glass and fill with champagne.
3. Garnish with a slice of orange; serve with a straw.

Mimosa

Mimosas are a perfect choice for your Easter brunch or dinner.

Ingredients:

- 3 oz. orange juice
- 3 oz. champagne, chilled
- 1 dash orange-flavored liqueur

Directions:

1. Pour orange juice into large, chilled wine glass.
2. Slowly pour in champagne, stirring gently.
3. Top with a dash of orange-flavored liqueur.

Portuguese Licoro

This homemade liqueur recipe originates from the island of St. Michael in the Azores.

Ingredients:

- 1 qt. whiskey
- ½ lemon
- 4½ c. sugar
- 1 qt. milk
- 6 sq. unsweetened chocolate (1 oz. each)
- 2 vanilla beans

Directions:

1. In gallon container combine whiskey, lemon half, sugar, milk, chocolate squares, and vanilla beans.

2. Keep at room temperature for 10 days, stirring once a day.
3. After 10 days, remove lemon half, remaining chocolate squares, and vanilla beans.
4. Insert coffee filter into large funnel.
5. Pour liquid through filter into gallon jug, changing filter as needed. (A clear yellow solution should result.)
6. If your solution is not clear, then filter until clear.
7. This liqueur can be stored in a sealed bottle at room temperature.

Bahama Mama

The Bahama Mama is a delicious adult drink, full of tropical flavor. It will add a touch of sunshine to your spring day!

Ingredients:

½ oz. rum
½ oz. coconut-flavored rum
½ oz. grenadine syrup
1 oz. orange juice
1 oz. pineapple juice
1 c. crushed ice

Directions:

1. Combine rums, grenadine, orange juice, pineapple juice, and crushed ice in electric blender.
2. Blend until consistency is slushy.
3. Pour into chilled tall glass to serve.

Yields: 1 serving.

Champagne Peach Punch

This looks nice in a punch bowl with a ring of ice with fruit or edible flowers frozen into it. Garnish with fruit or mint leaves.

Ingredients:

- 3 cans peach nectar (11½ oz. each)
- 1 can frozen orange juice concentrate (6 oz.)
- ¼ c. lemon juice
- ½ c. peach brandy
- ¼ c. grenadine syrup
- 1 bottle carbonated water (32 oz.)
- 3 bottles champagne (1½ pt. each)

Directions:

1. Chill all ingredients.
2. In large punch bowl combine peach nectar, orange juice concentrate, lemon juice, peach brandy, and grenadine.
3. Mix well; pour in carbonated water and champagne.

Bloody Mary

This is a great before-dinner drink, adding color to your menu.

Ingredients:

- 2 oz. vodka
  a few dashes Worcestershire sauce
  a few dashes hot sauce
  salt
  pepper
  twist of lime
  tomato juice
  ice
  celery sticks or asparagus spears

Directions:

1. Stir or shake vodka with sauces, spices, and twist of lime.
2. Pour into highball glass, add ice, and fill with tomato juice.
3. Garnish with celery stick or asparagus spear.

Vodka Blueberry Liqueur

This spirit takes some waiting time, but if you make it during blueberry season, you can enjoy the taste of fresh blueberries year round!

Ingredients:

1 c. sugar
2 c. vodka
3 c. fresh blueberries, cleaned, drained

Directions:

1. In 2-quart jar dissolve sugar in vodka.
2. Pour in blueberries and cover jar.
3. Store in cool, dark place for 2 months (refrigerator is okay).
4. Occasionally shake gently.
5. Strain and serve in cordial glasses, or if you prefer, over ice.

Wine Cooler

This is a refreshing spring wine cooler for your Easter dinner.

Ingredients:

½ oz. grapefruit juice
½ oz. pineapple juice
½ oz. lime juice
½ oz. lemon juice
4 oz. Chablis white wine
6 oz. lime soda

Directions:

1. Mix grapefruit, pineapple, lime, and lemon juices together in mixing glass.
2. Pour wine into tall wine glass, and add lime soda.
3. Add juice mix and serve.

Margarita

Margaritas are delicious. Make sure you use the best ingredients.

Ingredients for margarita:

1 lime wedge
1½ oz. tequila
½ oz. triple sec
1 oz. lime juice
coarse salt

Ingredients for frozen margarita:

1 lime wedge
3 oz. white tequila
1 oz. triple sec
2 oz. lime juice
1 c. crushed ice
coarse salt

Directions for margarita:

1. Rub rim of cocktail glass with lime wedge; dip rim in coarse salt.
2. Shake rest of ingredients with ice and strain into salt-rimmed glass; serve.

Spring Sangria

Sangria is a blend of fruits and wine that is very potent as well as flavorful.

Ingredients:

2 bottles red wine (750 ml. each)
4 c. rum, divided
4 c. orange juice, divided
1 c. sugar
1 pt. fresh strawberries
2 cans pineapple chunks in juice (20 oz. each)
1¼ jars maraschino cherries (10-oz. jars), drained

Directions:

1. In large pitcher mix red wine, 2 cups rum, 2 cups orange juice, and sugar.
2. Refrigerate at least 8 hours or overnight.
3. In large bowl mix strawberries, pineapple chunks, and maraschino cherries.
4. Cover with remaining 2 cups rum and remaining 2 cups orange juice.
5. Refrigerate at least 8 hours or overnight.
6. Drain fruit (reserve liquid if desired).
7. Mix fruit into pitcher with sangria to serve.

Amaretto

This recipe makes a delicious amaretto that is so close it is hard to tell it from the real thing.

Ingredients:

1	c. water
1	c. sugar
½	c. brown sugar, firmly packed
2	c. vodka
2	Tbs. almond extract
2	tsp. vanilla extract

Directions:

1. Combine water and sugars in saucepan over medium heat.
2. Heat until mixture is boiling and sugar is dissolved.
3. Remove pan from heat, and let mixture cool for 10 minutes.
4. Stir vodka, almond extract, and vanilla extract into mixture.
5. Store in sealed bottle.

Brandy Slush

This is a delicious, cool drink on a hot day. It is a hit at showers, garden parties, or when company comes.

Ingredients:

8	c. water
2	c. sugar
4	tea bags
2	cans frozen lemonade concentrate (12 oz. each)
2	cans frozen orange juice concentrate (12 oz. each)
13	oz. apricot brandy
	ginger ale, lemon-lime soda, or iced tea

Directions:

1. In large saucepan bring water to a boil; add sugar and stir until dissolved.
2. Add tea bags; let sit overnight at room temperature.
3. In large freezer-proof container, combine tea mixture with lemonade concentrate, orange juice concentrate, and apricot brandy.
4. Cover tightly and freeze, stirring every few hours until frozen.
5. To serve, place a few scoops of slush in a glass, then top glass with ginger ale, lemon-lime soda, or iced tea.

Strawberry Daiquiri

Strawberry daiquiris are a delightful drink and one of my favorites.

Ingredients:

2 oz. light rum
1 oz. lime juice
½ oz. superfine sugar
1 c. ice
5 strawberries, rinsed, hulled

Directions:

1. Combine all ingredients in blender at high speed.
2. Pour into Collins glass; serve with straw.

Salty Chihuahua

A Salty Chihuahua is a variation on the Salty Dog, and it is also fun to say.

Ingredients:

    1   wedge lime
    1½ oz. tequila
    5   oz. lemonade
        coarse salt
        ice

Directions:

1. Wet rim of an old-fashioned glass with lime wedge, then dip in salt.
2. Fill glass with ice.
3. Pour in tequila and lemonade.
4. Squeeze and drop in lime wedge.
5. Stir and serve.

White Russian

This white Russian is a light and soothing drink.

Ingredients:

    1½ oz. vodka
    ¾ oz. coffee-flavored liqueur
    ¾ oz. light cream or milk
       ice

Directions:

1. Mix vodka and liqueur together; float cream on top.
2. Add ice if desired.

Carrot Cake Martini

This one is just for the Easter bunny! Be sure to chill the glass and vodka.

Ingredients:

    1½ oz. vanilla vodka
    1   oz. butterscotch schnapps
    ½   oz. cinnamon schnapps
        cinnamon
        sugar
        sparkling water (optional)

Directions:

1. Dip rim of chilled martini glass in cinnamon and sugar.
2. Combine vodka, butterscotch schnapps, and cinnamon schnapps in cocktail shaker filled with ice cubes.
3. Shake well, strain into martini glass, and serve.
4. Top with optional water to lighten.

Banana Cream Pie Martini

This martini is like having dessert in a glass.

Ingredients:

    2   oz. premium vanilla vodka
    1   oz. banana liqueur
    1   oz. Irish Cream
        crushed ice

Directions:

1. Add vodka to shaker half filled with crushed ice, and shake a few times.
2. Add remaining alcohol and swirl.
3. Strain into cold/frozen martini glass.

Festival Information

Easter Festival of Running 2014
Isle of Man Easter Festival of Running, a great social and athletic weekend!!! For junior age groups, that age is at 1st September 2014. Minimum age is 15 for all the festival events. For veterans, age is on the first day of the Festival
i.e. 18th April.
Michelle Stevens, 15 Crovens Close
Governor's Hill, Douglas, Isle of Man, IM2 7AQ
For Easter Festival enquiries e-mail: easterfestival@manx.net
www.easterfestival.info

Community Easter Egg Hunt & Carnival
Easter egg hunts for infant, toddlers and children of ages 0-12. The Easter bunny will make an appearance. Bring a basket to collect the eggs!
Email: info@capitalchristian.com
Come join us at: 2760 E Fairview Ave, Meridian, ID 83646
Phone: 1(208) 888-1060

Zoo Boise Easter "Egg-stravaganza" Easter egg hunt
Join the Easter Bunny for fun activities including Egg Scrambles, photo ops, Egg toss, animal enriched activities and of course, the zoo. Admission
Join us at: 355 Julia Davis Drive, Boise, ID 83702
Phone: 1 (208) 384-4125x200

Springridge Farm Easter Festival
An Easter egg Hunt with the Easter Bunny
Families visiting the farm can also enjoy pony rides, the BBQ, New spring home décor and fresh baking!
Join us at: 7256 Bell School Line
Milton, Ontario L9T 2Y1
Phone: 1(905)878-4908
Email: info@springridgefarm.com

U.S. and Metric Measurement Charts

Here are some measurement equivalents to help you with exchanges. There was a time when many people thought the entire world would convert to the metric scale. While most of the world has, America still has not. Metric conversions in cooking are vitally important to preparing a tasty recipe. Here are simple conversion tables that should come in handy.

U.S. Measurement Equivalents

a few grains/pinch/dash (dry) = less than 1/8 teaspoon

a dash (liquid) = a few drops

3 teaspoons = 1 tablespoon

1/2 tablespoon = 1 1/2 teaspoons

1 tablespoon = 3 teaspoons

2 tablespoons = 1 fluid ounce

4 tablespoons = 1/4 cup

5 1/3 tablespoons = 1/3 cup

8 tablespoons = 1/2 cup

8 tablespoons = 4 fluid ounces

10 2/3 tablespoons = 2/3 cup

12 tablespoons = 3/4 cup

16 tablespoons = 1 cup

16 tablespoons = 8 fluid ounces

1/8 cup = 2 tablespoons

1/4 cup = 4 tablespoons

1/4 cup = 2 fluid ounces

1/3 cup = 5 tablespoons plus 1 teaspoon

1/2 cup = 8 tablespoons

1 cup = 16 tablespoons

1 cup = 8 fluid ounces

1 cup = 1/2 pint

2 cups = 1 pint

2 pints = 1 quart

4 quarts (liquid) = 1 gallon

8 quarts (dry) = 1 peck

4 pecks (dry) = 1 bushel

1 kilogram = approximately 2 pounds

1 liter=approximately 4 cups or 1quart

Approximate Metric Equivalents by Volume

U.S.Metric

1/4 cup = 60 milliliters

1/2 cup = 120 milliliters

1 cup = 230 milliliters

1 1/4 cups = 300 milliliters

1 1/2 cups = 360 milliliters

2 cups = 460 milliliters

2 1/2 cups = 600 milliliters

3 cups = 700 milliliters

4 cups (1 quart) = .95 liter

1.06 quarts = 1 liter

4 quarts (1 gallon) = 3.8 liters

Approximate Metric Equivalents by Weight

U.S. Metric

1/4 ounce = 7 grams

1/2 ounce = 14 grams

1 ounce = 28 grams

1 1/4 ounces = 35 grams

1 1/2 ounces = 40 grams

2 1/2 ounces = 70 grams

4 ounces = 112 grams

5 ounces = 140 grams

8 ounces = 228 grams

10 ounces = 280 grams

15 ounces = 425 grams

16 ounces (1 pound) = 454 grams

Glossary

Aerate: A synonym for sift; to pass ingredients through a fine-mesh device to break up large pieces and incorporate air into ingredients to make them lighter.

Al dente: "To the tooth," in Italian. The pasta is cooked just enough to maintain a firm, chewy texture.

Baste: To brush or spoon liquid fat or juices over meat during roasting to add flavor and prevent drying out.

Bias-slice: To slice a food crosswise at a 45-degree angle.

Bind: To thicken a sauce or hot liquid by stirring in ingredients such as eggs, flour, butter, or cream until it holds together.

Blackened: Popular Cajun-style cooking method. Seasoned foods are cooked over high heat in a super-heated heavy skillet until charred.

Blanch: To scald, as in vegetables being prepared for freezing; as in almonds so as to remove skins.

Blend: To mix or fold two or more ingredients together to obtain equal distribution throughout the mixture.

Braise: To brown meat in oil or other fat, and then cook slowly in liquid. The effect of braising is to tenderize the meat.

Bread: To coat food with crumbs (usually with soft or dry bread crumbs), sometimes seasoned.

Brown: To quickly sauté, broil, or grill either at the beginning or at the end of meal preparation, often to enhance flavor, texture, or eye appeal.

Brush: To use a pastry brush to coat a food such as meat or pastry with melted butter, glaze, or other liquid.

Butterfly: To cut open a food such as pork chops down the center without cutting all the way through, and then spread apart.

Caramelization: Browning sugar over a flame, with or without the addition of some water to aid the process. The temperature range in which sugar caramelizes is approximately 320 to 360 degrees F.

Clarify: To remove impurities from butter or stock by heating the liquid, then straining or skimming it.

Coddle: A cooking method in which foods (such as eggs) are put in separate containers and placed in a pan of simmering water for slow, gentle cooking.

Confit: To slowly cook pieces of meat in their own gently rendered fat.

Core: To remove the inedible center of fruits such as pineapples.

Cream: To beat vegetable shortening, butter, or margarine, with or without sugar, until light and fluffy. This process traps in air bubbles, later used to create height in cookies and cakes.

Crimp: To create a decorative edge on a pie crust. On a double pie crust, this also seals the edges together.

Curd: A custard-like pie or tart filling flavored with juice and zest of citrus fruit, usually lemon, although lime and orange may also be used.

Curdle: To cause semisolid pieces of coagulated protein to develop in food, usually as a result of the addition of an acid substance or the overheating of milk or egg-based sauces.

Custard: A mixture of beaten egg, milk, and possibly other ingredients such as sweet or savory flavorings, which are cooked with gentle heat, often in a water bath or double boiler. As pie filling, the custard is frequently cooked and chilled before being layered into a baked crust.

Deglaze: To add liquid to a pan in which foods have been fried or roasted, in order to dissolve the caramelized juices stuck to the bottom of the pan.

Dot: To sprinkle food with small bits of an ingredient such as butter to allow for even melting.

Dredge: To sprinkle lightly and evenly with sugar or flour. A dredger has holes pierced on the lid to sprinkle evenly.

Drippings: The liquids left in the bottom of a roasting or frying pan after meat is cooked. Drippings are generally used for gravies and sauces.

Drizzle: To pour a liquid such as a sweet glaze or melted butter in a slow, light trickle over food.

Dust: To sprinkle food lightly with spices, sugar, or flour for a light coating.

Egg Wash: A mixture of beaten eggs (yolks, whites, or whole eggs) and either milk or water. Used to coat cookies and other baked goods to give them a shine when baked.

Emulsion: A mixture of liquids, one being a fat or oil and the other being water based so that tiny globules of one are suspended in the other. This may involve the use of stabilizers, such as egg or custard. Emulsions may be temporary or permanent.

Entrée: A French term that originally referred to the first course of a meal, served after the soup and before the meat courses. In the United States, it refers to the main dish of a meal.

Fillet: To remove the bones from meat or fish for cooking.

Filter: To remove lumps, excess liquid or impurities by passing through paper or cheesecloth.

Firm-Ball Stage: In candy making, the point at which boiling syrup dropped in cold water forms a ball that is compact yet gives slightly to the touch.

Flambé: To ignite a sauce or other liquid so that it flames.

Flan: An open pie filled with sweet or savory ingredients; also, a Spanish dessert of baked custard covered with caramel.

Flute: To create a decorative scalloped or undulating edge on a pie crust or other pastry.

Fricassee: Usually a stew in which the meat is cut up, lightly cooked in butter, and then simmered in liquid until done.

Frizzle: To cook thin slices of meat in hot oil until crisp and slightly curly.

Ganache: A rich chocolate filling or coating made with chocolate, vegetable shortening, and possibly heavy cream. It can coat cakes or cookies and be used as a filling for truffles.

Glaze: A liquid that gives an item a shiny surface. Examples are fruit jams that have been heated or chocolate thinned with melted vegetable shortening. Also, to cover a food with such a liquid.

Gratin: To bind together or combine food with a liquid such as cream, milk, béchamel sauce, or tomato sauce in a shallow dish. The mixture is then baked until cooked and set.

Hard-Ball Stage: In candy making, the point at which syrup has cooked long enough to form a solid ball in cold water.

Hull (also husk): To remove the leafy parts of soft fruits, such as strawberries or blackberries.

Infusion: To extract flavors by soaking them in liquid heated in a covered pan. The term also refers to the liquid resulting from this process.

Jerk or Jamaican Jerk Seasoning: A dry mixture of various spices such as chilies, thyme, garlic, onions, and cinnamon or cloves used to season meats such as chicken or pork.

Julienne: To cut into long, thin strips.

Jus: The natural juices released by roasting meats.

Larding: To inset strips of fat into pieces of meat, so that the braised meat stays moist and juicy.

Marble: To gently swirl one food into another.

Marinate: To combine food with aromatic ingredients to add flavor.

Meringue: Egg whites beaten until they are stiff, then sweetened. It can be used as the topping for pies or baked as cookies.

Mull: To slowly heat cider with spices and sugar.

Parboil: To partly cook in a boiling liquid.

Peaks: The mounds made in a mixture. For example, egg white that has been whipped to stiffness. Peaks are "stiff" if they stay upright or "soft" if they curl over.

Pesto: A sauce usually made of fresh basil, garlic, olive oil, pine nuts, and cheese. The ingredients are finely chopped and then mixed, uncooked, with pasta. Generally, the term refers to any uncooked sauce made of finely chopped herbs and nuts.

Pipe: To force a semisoft food through a bag (either a pastry bag or a plastic bag with one corner cut off) to decorate food.

Pressure Cooking: To cook using steam trapped under a locked lid to produce high temperatures and achieve fast cooking time.

Purée: To mash or sieve food into a thick liquid.

Ramekin: A small baking dish used for individual servings of sweet and savory dishes.

Reduce: To cook liquids down so that some of the water evaporates.

Refresh: To pour cold water over freshly cooked vegetables to prevent further cooking and to retain color.

Roux: A cooked paste usually made from flour and butter, used to thicken sauces.

Sauté: To cook foods quickly in a small amount of oil in a skillet or sauté pan over direct heat.

Scald: To heat a liquid, usually a dairy product, until it almost boils.

Sear: To seal in a meat's juices by cooking it quickly using very high heat.

Seize: To form a thick, lumpy mass when melted (usually applies to chocolate).

Sift: To remove large lumps from a dry ingredient such as flour or confectioners' sugar by passing it through a fine mesh.

This process also incorporates air into the ingredients, making them lighter.

Simmer: To cook food in a liquid at a low enough temperature that small bubbles begin to break the surface.

Steam: To cook over boiling water in a covered pan. This method keeps foods' shape, texture, and nutritional value intact better than methods such as boiling.

Steep: To soak dry ingredients (tea leaves, ground coffee, herbs, spices, etc.) in liquid until the flavor is infused into the liquid.

Stewing: To brown small pieces of meat, poultry, or fish, then simmer them with vegetables or other ingredients in enough liquid to cover them, usually in a closed pot on the stove, in the oven, or with a slow cooker.

Thin: To reduce a mixture's thickness with the addition of more liquid.

Truss: To use string, skewers, or pins to hold together a food to maintain its shape while it cooks (usually applied to meat or poultry).

Unleavened: Baked goods that contain no agents to give them volume, such as baking powder, baking soda, or yeast.

Vinaigrette: A general term referring to any sauce made with vinegar, oil, and seasonings.

Zest: The thin, brightly colored outer part of the rind of citrus fruits. It contains volatile oils, used as a flavoring.

Recipe Index of Easter Delights

Reader Feedback Form

Dear Reader,

We are very interested in what our readers think. Please fill in the form below and return it to:

Whispering Pine Press International, Inc.
c/o Easter Delights Cookbook
P.O. Box 214, Spokane Valley, WA 99037-0214 USA
Phone: (509) 928-8700 | Fax: (509) 922-9949
Email: sales@WhisperingPinePress.com
Publisher Website: www.WhisperingPinePress.com
Book Website: www.EasterDelightsCookbook.com

Name: _____

Address: _____

City, St., Zip: _____

Phone/Fax: (____) _____ / (____) _____

Email: _____

Comments/Suggestions: _____

_____

_____

_____

_____

A great deal of care and attention has been exercised in the creation of this book. Designing a great cookbook that is original, fun, and easy to use has been a job that required many hours of diligence, creativity, and research. Although we strive to make this book completely error free, errors and discrepancies may not be completely excluded. If you come across any errors or discrepancies, please make a note of them and send them to our publishing office. We are constantly updating our manuscripts, eliminating errors, and improving quality.

Please contact us at the address above.

About the Cookbook Delights Series

The *Cookbook Delights Series* includes many different topics and themes. If you have a passion for food and wish to know more information about different foods, then this series of cookbooks will be beneficial to you. Each book features a different type of food, such as avocados, strawberries, huckleberries, salmon, vegetarian, lentils, almonds, cherries, coconuts, lemons, and many, many more.

The *Cookbook Delights Series* not only includes cookbooks about individual foods but also includes several holiday-themed cookbooks. Whatever your favorite holiday may be, chances are we have a cookbook with recipes designed with that holiday in mind. Some examples include *Halloween Delights, Thanksgiving Delights, Christmas Delights, Valentine Delights, Mother's Day Delights, St. Patrick's Day Delights,* and *Easter Delights.*

Each cookbook is designed for easy use and is organized into alphabetical sections. Over 250 recipes are included along with other interesting facts, folklore, and history of the featured food or theme. Each book comes with a beautiful full-color cover, ordering information, and a list of other upcoming books in the series.

Note cards, bookmarks, and a daily journal have been printed and are available to go along with each cookbook. You may view the entire line of cookbooks, journals, cards, posters, puzzles, and bookmarks by visiting our websites at www.CookBookDelights. net and www.EasterDelights.com, or you can email us with your questions and your comments to: sales@WhisperingPinePress. com.

Please ask your local bookstore to carry these sets of books.

To order, please contact:

Whispering Pine Press International, Inc.
c/o Easter Delights Cookbook
P.O. Box 214, Spokane Valley, WA 99037-0214 USA
Phone: (509) 9928-8700| Fax: (509) 922-9949
Email: sales@WhisperingPinePress.com
Publisher Website: www.WhisperingPinePress.com
Book Website: www.EasterDelightsCookbook.com
SAN 253-200X

We Invite You to Join the Whispering Pine Press International, Inc., Book Club!

Whispering Pine Press International, Inc.
c/o Easter Delights Cookbook
P.O. Box 214, Spokane Valley, WA 99037-0214 USA
Phone: (509) 928-8700 | Fax: (509) 922-9949
Email: sales@WhisperingPinePress.com
Publisher Website: www.WhisperingPinePress.com
Book Website: www.EasterDelightsCookbook.com

Buy 11 books and get the next one free, based on the average price of the first eleven purchased.

How the club works:

Simply use the order form below and order books from our catalog. You can buy just one at a time or all eleven at once. After the first eleven books are purchased, the next one is free. Please add shipping and handling as listed on this form. There are no purchase requirements at any time during your membership. Free book credit is based on the average price of the first eleven books purchased.

Join today! Pick your books and mail in the form today!

Yes! I want to join the Whispering Pine Press International, Inc., Book Club! Enroll me and send the books indicated below.

Title   Price

1. _____

2. _____

3. _____

4. _____

5. _____

6. _____

7. _____

8. _____

9. _____

10. _____

Free Book Title: _____

Free Book Price: _____Avg. Price: _____ Total Price: _____

Credit for the free book is based on the average price of the first 11 books purchased.

(Circle one) Check | Visa | MasterCard | Discover | American Express

Credit Card #: _____ Expiration Date: _____

Name: _____

Address: _____

City: _____State: _____Country: _____

Zip/Postal: _____Phone: (_____) _____

Email: _____

Signature_____

Whispering Pine Press International, Inc. Fundraising Opportunities

Fundraising cookbooks are proven moneymakers and great keepsake providers for your group. Whispering Pine Press International, Inc. offers a very special personalized cookbook fundraising program that encourages success to organizations all across the USA.

Our prices are competitive and fair. Currently, we offer a special of 100 books with many free features and excellent customer service. Any purchase you make is guaranteed first-rate.

Flexibility is not a problem. If you have special needs, we guarantee our cooperation in meeting each of them. Our goal is to create a cookbook that goes beyond your expectations. We have the confidence and a record that promises continual success.

Another great fundraising program is the *Cookbook Delights Series* Program. With cookbook orders of 50 copies or more, your organization receives a huge discount, making for a prompt and lucrative solution.

We also specialize in assisting group fundraising – Christian, community, nonprofit, and academic among them. If you are struggling for a new idea, something that will enhance your success and broaden your appeal, Whispering Pine Press International, Inc., can help.

For more information, write, phone, or fax to:

Whispering Pine Press International, Inc.
P.O. Box 214, Spokane Valley, WA 99037-0214 USA
Phone: (509) 928-8700 | Fax: (509) 922-9949
Email: sales@WhisperingPinePress.com
Publisher Website: www.WhisperingPinePress.com
Book Website: www.EasterDelightsCookbook.com
SAN 253-200X

Personalized and/or Translated Order Form for Any Book by Whispering Pine Press International, Inc.

Dear Readers:

If you or your organization wishes to have this book or any other of our books personalized, we will gladly accommodate your needs. For instance, if you would like to change the names of the characters in a book to the names of the children in your family or Sunday school class, we would be happy to work with you on such a project. We can add more information of your choosing and customize this book especially for your family, group, or organization.

We are also offering an option of translating your book into another language. Please fill out the form below telling us exactly how you would like us to personalize your book.

Please send your request to:

Whispering Pine Press International, Inc.
P.O. Box 214, Spokane Valley, WA 99037-0214 USA
Phone: (509) 928-8700 | Fax: (509) 922-9949
Email: sales@WhisperingPinePress.com
Publisher Website: www.WhisperingPinePress.com
Book Website: www.EasterDelightsCookbook.com

Person/Organization placing request: _____

Date_____ Phone: (____) _____

Address_____ Fax: (____) _____

City_____ State_____ Zip: _____

Language of the book: _____

Please explain your request in detail: _____

_____

_____

_____

Easter Delights Cookbook
A Collection of Easter Recipes
How to Order

Get your additional copies of this book by returning an order form and your check, money order, or credit card information to:

Whispering Pine Press International, Inc.
P.O. Box 214, Spokane Valley, WA 99037-0214 USA
Phone: (509) 928-8700 | Fax: (509) 922-9949
Email: sales@WhisperingPinePress.com
Publisher Website: www.WhisperingPinePress.com
Book Website: www.EasterDelightsCookbook.com

Customer Name: _____

Address: _____

City, St., Zip: _____

Phone/Fax: _____

Email: _____

- -

Please send me _____ copies of _____ _____
_____ at $_____ per copy
and $4.95 for shipping and handling per book, plus $2.95 each for additional books. Enclosed is my check, money order, or charge my account for $_____.

☐ Check   ☐ Money Order   ☐ Credit Card

(*Circle One*) MasterCard | Discover | Visa | American Express
☐☐☐☐   ☐☐☐☐   ☐☐☐☐   ☐☐☐☐

Expiration Date: _____

_____
Signature

_____
Print Name

321

Whispering Pine Press International, Inc. Order Form

Gift-wrapping, Autographing, and Inscription

We are proud to offer personal autographing by the author. For a limited time this service is absolutely free!
Gift-wrapping is also available for $4.95 per item.

1. Sold To

Name: _____
Street/Route: _____
_____
City: _____
State: _____ Zip: _____
Country: _____
Gift message: _____
_____
Email address: _____
Daytime Phone: (_ _) _ _ _-_ _ _ _
*Necessary for verifying orders
Home Phone: (_ _) _ _ _-_ _ _ _
Fax: (_ _) _ _ _-_ _ _ _

2. Ship To

☐ Is this a new or corrected address?

☐ Alternative Shipping Address

☐ Mailing Address

Name: _____
Address: _____
_____
City: _____
State: _____ Zip: _____
Country: _____
Email address: _____

3. Items Ordered

ISBN # /Item #	Size	Color	Qty.	Title or Description	Price	Total

4. Method Of Payment

International, Inc. (No Cash or COD's)

☐ Visa ☐ MasterCard ☐ Discover ☐ American Express ☐ Check/Money Order
Please make it payable to Whispering Pine Press International, Inc. (No Cash or COD's)

Account Number   Expiration Date
                                   _____ / _____
                                   Month Year

☐☐☐☐ ☐☐☐☐ ☐☐☐☐ ☐☐☐☐

Signature_____
            Cardholder's signature
Printed Name_____
            Please print name of cardholder
Address of Cardholder_____

Subtotal	
Gift wrap $4.95 Each	
For delivery in WA add 8.7% sales tax.	
Shipping See chart at left	
6. Total	

5. Shipping & Handling

Continental US

US Postal Ground: For books please add $4.95 for the first book and $2.95 each for additional books.
All non-book items, add 15% of the Subtotal.
Please allow 1-4 weeks for delivery.
US Postal Air: Please add $15.00 shipping and handling.
Please allow 1-3 days for delivery.
Alaska, Hawaii, and the US Territories By Ship:
Please add 10% shipping and handling
(minimum charge $15.00).

Please
By Air: Please add 12% shipping and handling (minimum charge $15.00).
Please allow 2 –6 weeks for delivery.
International By Ship: Please add 10% shipping and handling (minimum charge $15.00).
Please allow 6-12 weeks for delivery.
By Air: Please add 12% shipping and handling (minimum charge $15.00).
Please allow 2-6 weeks for delivery.
FedEx Shipments: Add $5.00 to the above airmail charges for overnight delivery.

Shop Online:
www.whisperingpinepress.com
Fax orders to: (509) 922-9949

Whispering Pine Press International, Inc.
P.O. Box 214
Spokane Valley, WA 99037-0214 USA
Phone: (509) 928-8700 • Fax: (509) 922-9949
Email: sales@whisperingpinepress.com
Website: www.whisperingpinepress.com

About the Author and Cook

Karen Jean Matsko Hood has always enjoyed cooking, baking, and experimenting with recipes. At this time Hood is working to complete a series of cookbooks that blends her skills and experience in cooking and entertaining. Hood entertains large groups of people and especially enjoys designing creative menus with holiday, international, ethnic, and regional themes.

Hood is publishing a cookbook series entitled the *Cookbook Delights Series*, in which each cookbook emphasizes a different food ingredient or theme. The first cookbook in the series is *Apple Delights Cookbook*. Hood is working to complete another series of cookbooks titled *Hood and Matsko Family Cookbooks*, which includes many recipes handed down from her family heritage and others that have emerged from more current family traditions. She has been invited to speak on talk radio shows on various topics, and favorite recipes from her cookbooks have been prepared on local television programs.

Hood was born and raised in Great Falls, Montana. As an undergraduate, she attended the College of St. Benedict in St. Joseph, Minnesota, and St. John's University in Collegeville, Minnesota. She attended the University of Great Falls in Great Falls, Montana. Hood received a B.S. Degree in Natural Science from the College of St. Benedict and minored in both Psychology and Secondary Education. Upon her graduation, Hood and her husband taught science and math on the island of St. Croix in the U.S. Virgin Islands. Hood has completed postgraduate classes at the University of Iowa in Iowa City, Iowa. In May 2001, she completed her Master's Degree in Pastoral Ministry at Gonzaga University in Spokane, Washington. She has taken postgraduate classes at Lewis and Clark College on the North Idaho college campus in Coeur d'Alene, Idaho, Taylor University in Fort Wayne, Indiana, Spokane Falls Community College, Spokane Community College, Washington State University, University of Washington, and Eastern Washington University. Hood is working on research projects to complete her Ph.D. in Leadership Studies at Gonzaga University in Spokane, Washington.

Hood resides in Greenacres, Washington, along with her husband, many of her sixteen children, and foster children. Her interests include writing, research, and teaching. She previously has volunteered as a court advocate in the Spokane juvenile court system for abused and neglected children. Hood is a literary advocate for youth and adults. Her hobbies include cooking, baking, collecting, photography, indoor and outdoor gardening, farming, and the cultivation of unusual flowering plants and orchids. She enjoys raising several specialty breeds of animals including Babydoll

Southdown, Friesen, and Icelandic sheep, Icelandic horses, bichons frisés, cockapoos, Icelandic sheepdogs, a Newfoundland, a Rottweiler, a variety of Nubian and fainting goats, and a few rescue cats. Hood also enjoys bird-watching and finds all aspects of nature precious.

She demonstrates a passionate appreciation of the environment and a respect for all life. She also invites you to visit her websites:

www.KarenJeanMatskoHood.com
www.KarenJeanMatskoHoodBookstore.com
www.KarenJeanMatskoHoodBlog.com
www.KarensKidsBooks.com
www.KarensTeenBooks.com

www.HoodFamilyBlog.com
www.HoodFamily.com

www.ingramcontent.com/pod-product-compliance
Lightning Source LLC
Chambersburg PA
CBHW031235090426
42742CB00007B/208